THE HUMANIST SOCIETY

The Social Blueprint for Self-Actualization

Joseph Sassoon

THE HUMANIST SOCIETY
THE SOCIAL BLUEPRINT FOR SELF-ACTUALIZATION

iUniverse books may be ordered through booksellers or by contacting:

iUniverse
1663 Liberty Drive
Bloomington, IN 47403
www.iuniverse.com
1-800-Authors (1-800-288-4677)

ISBN: 978-1-4917-3148-2 (sc)
ISBN: 978-1-4917-3149-9 (hc)
ISBN: 978-1-4917-3150-5 (e)

Library of Congress Control Number: 2014906386

Printed in the United States of America.

iUniverse rev. date: 10/04/2016

CONTENTS

PREFACE

I was born in Baghdad and grew up there but left at the age of fifteen, never to return. And I was not alone. This was the end of my community's long sojourn in Mesopotamia, a sojourn that dated back approximately twenty-six centuries. No wonder I was always fascinated by the biblical story about Jews arriving as exiles in Babylon. They were my direct ancestors. Their history—my history—raises a question that Jews have always asked: How could such a small community have survived for so long, both there and elsewhere, at the mercy of bigger and stronger ones that were not always friendly? In other words, why did we not assimilate and disappear as so many other communities did?

Seen from a slightly different perspective, however, the question looks like this: what accounts for the rise and fall of so many civilizations that were more powerful politically?

As a child, I found insight in the ideas of my great-great-uncle, Ben Ish Hai (many of whose books still sell in Jewish bookstores around the world).[1] From the late nineteenth century to the early twentieth, he preached at the Great Synagogue in Baghdad. One motif that reappeared in his sermons was that the Babylonian Talmud, inspired by God and transmitted in oral and then written forms, reveals not only genuine compassion but also deep insight into human nature—what we call human values. This insight, applied to behavior in everyday life, helped save our community from assimilation and disappearance. Jews, including free thinkers, valued their way of life too highly to discard it and join other communities, despite stiff competition and occasional hostility from those other communities.

Ben Ish Hai added that Judaism would eventually become the universal religion, because it corresponds more closely than any other to human nature. Judaism must be preserved, therefore, as a testimony to God's will that the people of Israel spread his divine message. This would set an example and encourage all communities to reach the highest level of achievement. If the biblical tradition works for Jews under varying conditions of stress and liberty, after all, why not for all peoples?

As a Jew, of course, I am inclined to agree with him. But I am not a missionary for Judaism. I am a missionary for humanism, which just happens to resemble a secularized version of Judaism. People have come to humanism from many worldviews, but I have come to it from the Jewish one. Judaism was not the only thing, however, that brought me to humanism. As an adolescent in Iraq, I experienced despotism. And avoiding that is my major aim in this book.

Fortunately, my father could afford to send me abroad to study. I finished university in the United States, with a degree in business administration. In that setting, though, I became interested in world federalism—a method of ensuring peace with justice—by attending the lectures of regular members and leaders of the American World Federalist movement. Although I agreed enthusiastically with the aims of that movement, I did not agree with the proposed means. Their plan called for a federation between democratic states (such as the United States) and authoritarian ones (such as the former Soviet Union) under some vague conditions. I did not think that this would work. A union of ideologically diverse nations, I believed, would be impossible. To achieve a world federation would require a single ideology— not one that would be imposed by the strongest powers, but one that would be based on human nature and therefore beyond the opportunism resulting from the self-interest of this or that powerful country.

I came to believe, therefore, that the prerequisite for a world government would be a universal worldview—that is, one that would be derived directly from nature. It would require two methods, the carrot and the stick, to ensure not only security but also better lives for all members.

After graduation, I joined my family, which had already migrated to Canada. We were all glad to be living in a free and democratic country. I joined my father's newly established real estate development company. This enabled me, after years of hard work, to have an independent income. And that, in turn, allowed me the time to concentrate on world federalism and also, as it turned out, on self-actualization.

Only two years after his arrival in Canada, unfortunately, my father died. As the eldest of four siblings, I was now responsible not only for the family business but also for the care of my mother, two sisters, and a six-year-old brother. All this in a new country.

Meanwhile, I read *Human Nature in the Light of Psychopathology*, by Kurt Goldstein.[2] He discussed self-actualization as a universal drive. Despite my own grieving, I found that Goldstein's theory revived my hope for a universal civilization. But I still needed to know how this drive worked. After studying that problem for several decades, admittedly as an amateur, I was able to publish my first book. My topic was the anatomy and technology of self-actualization.

This new volume is the second in what I hope will become a trilogy on the social conditions that will be necessary to achieve the self-actualization of the greatest number of people. A third volume, which will establish the conditions required to bring about a humanist world federalism, will follow.

My original aim in trying to discover a universal moral code, derived from Goldstein's theory of self-actualization, has led to discoveries that could unify, simplify, and entirely change the social sciences. I would say that Goldstein's original theory and its extension into the unified theory of motivation (see appendix A) has in effect cut the Gordian knot that has prevented them from being true sciences.

Besides the technology of self-actualization, I propose a moral code that is derived from nature (sometimes through religion). The unified theory of motivation covers all activities and their precise effects on self-actualization: knowledge, education, work, family, social life, food, sex, physical safety, and health. It includes all reactions, those that seek to avoid suffering or failure and those that would cause deleterious behaviors.

Among the most important achievements of this theory is the social order that it promotes, relying on the overall drive toward self-actualization. That is the major topic of this book.

Last but not least is a theory of democracy in accord with the humanist worldview. Without the latter—majority rule, elections, and so on—would either not work or lead to mob rule (as the Greeks and the American founding fathers predicted).

Goldstein's original theory and my own extension of it would make possible simplified social sciences. These would solve most or all human problems, creating a sane and secure international order and thus laying the groundwork for a democratic form of world federalism.

INTRODUCTION

Leonardo da Vinci rejected Greek and Roman philosophies because they were not based on observation. I was forced to reject these and all other philosophies because they are not based on a natural law and therefore are not beyond manipulation for personal or collective benefit. I believe that conflicting philosophies not only divide people but also fail to offer adequate solutions to crucial modern problems—those that threaten human freedom and even human survival. Worst of all, they have produced no common method of defining good and evil.

This somber picture changed dramatically, in my opinion, with the advent of humanist psychology. It posits an overall drive toward self-actualization as the only all-inclusive constant in human affairs. It is instinctive and therefore universal in humans. It stands as the single invariable feature of human existence for all matters of human affairs, I believe, and thus offers a method for solving all problems in relation to that single invariable.

In *Man the Unknown*, Alexis Carrel asserted that ignorance of human nature is the single most serious lack in our knowledge of the world and the single greatest hazard for our continued existence in it. He warned, even before the nuclear age, that all of our material or technological advances could lead to the end of civilization. We need not only more knowledge of human nature, he added, but also the kind of social organization that would accommodate it.[3]

The idea of self-actualization was developed by Kurt Goldstein[4] (1878–1965), Abraham Maslow[5] (1908–1970), and others. It presents the natural paradigm to which we can refer all problems and find the best solutions, ones that are based on biological needs as known from empirical evidence. I consider this a major breakthrough in the field of psychology and believe that it has the potential, through humanism, for solving major problems that have so far gone unsolved. Humanism begins with individual, because that is the irreducible core of every human being. As Goldstein hypothesized, after all, everyone is governed by the overall drive toward self-actualization.

The next task was mine: to discover, through observation over several decades, how that system actually works—which is to say, how the parts work together in the interest of self-actualization. I published my findings in the first volume of this trilogy.[6] This book is the second volume, and its goal is to show how we can organize society so that the greatest number of people will achieve self-actualization. That is what humanism is all about.

This work might seem audacious to some, but I find it necessary and timely. Like any work that breaks new ground, it cannot be perfect. I believe, nevertheless, that we must begin to work on a topic of such far-reaching implications.

In this book, I suggest that a humanist society would be one function of self-actualization. In other words, it would provide the highest level of self-actualization for the highest number of people.[7] Even though I will articulate a philosophy, therefore, my philosophy has an empirical basis and does not rely on the distorting lens of any other philosophy—or, for that matter, any theology or ideology. This book is less about society itself, in other words, than about how society can satisfy—should satisfy— the striving of everyone for self-actualization.

I am addressing primarily those who feel the need for an entirely new social organization, one that fosters self-actualization for everyone or at least almost everyone. This is a basic right, I suggest, because it is derived from human nature itself—which explains the name "humanism."

Some societies are better than others from this point of view. At one end of the spectrum are democracies; at the other end are dictatorships. Both are what social scientists call "ideal types," the humanist society and the antihumanist society. No society ever attains perfection in representing either end of the continuum, although some have come very close to perfect antihumanism. For the sake of convenience, though, I will refer to societies moving in the direction of greater humanism as *humanist* and those moving in the opposite direction as *authoritarian* societies. The former would be both rational and democratic, because they would follow the contours and therefore the guidelines of human nature.

There is a clear and unmistakable difference between humanist and authoritarian societies. This book is about revealing one and exposing the other. Humanist societies foster self-actualization, democracy, liberty, human rights, secularity, empathy, longevity, and opposition to injustice everywhere. All of these characteristics are measurable.

Authoritarian societies, by contrast, foster only low levels of the same characteristics. Many of them have high levels of poverty and corruption. Some of them—Nazi Germany, for instance—are prosperous, but the drive to expand leads them to war. These, of course, are the most dangerous authoritarian societies. From my point of view, humanist societies are the only healthy ones; authoritarian societies are pathological to the extent that they violate human nature—that is, deny basic human needs.

In the first volume of this trilogy, I presented a unified theory of motivation, my extension of Goldstein's theory of self-actualization. I noted that the word *self-actualization* was misleading, because it implies some form of selfishness: placing oneself apart from society or even above it. According to Maslow, however, personal self-actualization always requires a social context. Therefore, I suggest, it requires the self-actualization of society as a whole. The individual is very much involved with the well-being of society, because the self-actualization of one depends on that of the other. To put it another way, self-actualization involves identification with and empathy for all other selves.[8] This is what Maslow discovered in his study of healthy achievers. In contemporary parlance, I would refer to the *synergy* between every individual and society.

To avoid confusion about the word *self-actualization*, I refer instead sometimes to *entelechy*. That word, derived from the Greek, refers to the natural motivation of every living thing. The entelechial process therefore refers to the coordination of all instincts so that they work together as a unit. (For the details on how specific instincts do so, on the unified theory of motivations, see appendix A.)

A humanist society would therefore be a function of the entelechial process. Creating this kind of society would be an empirical project and subject to verification at every step. We can ignore the entelechial process and bear the consequences, of course, just as we can ignore any other natural process.

Historically, moral codes have relied primarily on religion. Some religions have promoted humanist codes and others antihumanist ones. Religion remains the primary control mechanism for most societies, which is one reason for its continuing importance to the people who control them. In chapters 1 and 2, therefore, I will discuss the crucial role of religion in either supporting or suppressing democracy.

In chapter 3, I will turn to science and its role in proclaiming and enforcing the humanist values that forms the backbone of democracy. By these values, I refer to those that rely not only on human nature but also on religion—to the extent that they can be translated into equivalent secular terms. My primary aim is to give secular science the lead in promoting democracy. It contains the humanist code, after all, and that contains the rules that would be necessary to bring about a humanist society. But my secondary aim is to foster the humanist values that can be found within all religions when translated into secular terms.

In chapters 4 through 7, I will discuss various aspects of democracy. One is the principle of social devolution, which is the topic of chapter 4. By that, I refer to why and how democracy declines when separated from its humanist sources. Chapter 5 is about the structure of democracy. My aim there is to show that values, taken together, form the fixed guiding mechanism of democracy. All other aspects are variables, which means that they are subject to trial and error.

Chapter 6 deals with the evolution of democracy from its primitive but pioneering past in ancient Athens to the constitutional present. Of particular interest to me are ways in which activists, legislators, and jurists have begun to interpret law. I suggest that we will have to rescue democracy from them before attaining the future fulfillment of democracy. By establishing humanism, we would put democracy on a firm foundation—one like that of the natural sciences.

Chapter 7, therefore, deals with legal interpretation from a specifically humanist perspective—one that relies exclusively on empirical evidence.

In chapters 8 through 10, I will turn to more specific topics: economics, education, and journalism from a humanist perspective. The aim of humanist economics would be to distribute wealth so that it fosters the entelechial process of as many people as possible. The aim of humanist education would be to promote democracy early in every child's life. Every student would have to learn, no matter what the pedagogical vocabulary, that the entelechial process is rooted in human nature and that only humanism makes it possible. Every student would have to learn about a basic link between that process and human rights. As a result, every student would realize that the only correct interpretation of any religion is a humanist one.

Journalism is another powerful instrument. Journalists are responsible not only for presenting facts correctly but also for promoting a humanist bias, because humanism is the only legitimate reference point for all true or useful information.

In the second part of this book, I will discuss pathology. Chapter 11 defines evil in terms of the entelechial process and the humanist code. I suggest that most forms of evil are manageable. The most dangerous form of evil is governmental. I am referring here to the totalitarianism of modern dictatorships, which not only violates basic human rights but also, given weapons of mass destruction, endangers human survival. Chapter 12 deals exclusively with the evils of dictatorship. A humanist analysis of motivation would make it possible to isolate and ultimately eliminate that pathology without affecting the rise of a humanist society.

In the epilogue, I will discuss history from a humanist perspective. Despite the setbacks, I see progress—that is, the movement toward world federalism based on the universal adoption of humanism.

Before concluding, I should explain the two-dimensional gestalt system, which I have developed in order to separate ends and means in defining important projects such as democracy. One example of confusion over ends and means would be the Iraq War. From a humanist point of view, the United States was correct in attacking the country and removing its dictator, who had become a menace to world peace. But trying to force democracy on people who were not ready for it was another matter. The result was a hybrid democracy, not a true democracy. Giving Iraqis the right to vote was merely the means to a greater end, not an end in itself. Iraqis voted, to be sure, but many of them failed to understand human rights—an essential feature of democracy. In my opinion, they would have been better served by a benign dictator, someone under American influence and backed by American power. Democracy cannot be imposed by force, but dictatorship can be. Democracy can be reliably supported only by people who understand it. (See appendix B.) To do that, the people must learn that the source of human rights is human nature—the entelechial process.

With all this in mind, I have adopted a two-dimensional gestalt formulation. Doing so entails the clear separation of ends from means. In this book, I have separated the two dimensions by colons. Here is an example: $P = A: B$. P is for project; A is the end; B is the means. This equation applies to every act. Moreover, it indicates the implications of every act on the entelechial process.

Chapter 1

RELIGION AND DEMOCRACY

Humanism, I believe, is the oxygen of democracy. It motivates people to find the best social environment in which to develop both individual and collective potential. Humanist values are the only ones that can support democracy on a permanent basis. But religion has so far supplied the values of all societies, both democratic and nondemocratic. Clearly, then, religion and democracy are closely related.

To me, as a religious humanist, it is obvious that democracy—to the extent that it follows and promotes the entelechial process—conveys the will of God and contains the primary inner bond between the divine and the human. Self-actualization, as Abraham Maslow has shown, leads to deep spirituality. But we must distinguish spirituality from organized religion.[9]

Spirituality is instinctive and expresses a universal hunger for union with the nonhuman or superhuman. But I believe also that organized religion does not always foster spirituality. Why not? Because it has functions in addition to fostering spirituality. Organized religion originated as a way of organizing society.[10]

By definition, it has social, political, and economic functions as well as spiritual ones.

From my point of view as a religious humanist, the entelechial process not only deepens spirituality but also fosters maturity. It represents the natural instincts of healthy people and defines their functions within society. And it works on a microlevel as well as a macrolevel. Democracy is the only political system that fosters the entelechial process. Moreover, it is the only one that fosters the peaceful coexistence of countries—at least democratic countries.

But only a few people understand how democracy works, and they cannot maintain it all alone. They need the consent, supervision, and critical backing of society as a whole—that is, of a humanist society. Without the full participation of everyone, democracy quickly becomes corrupt. A small ruling class takes advantage of public ignorance and indifference. Eventually, to secure public order, society resorts to some form of absolute rule.

This is exactly what happened to the democracy of ancient Athens. Aristotle and Plato maintained that the system—which, in my opinion, lacked the essential ingredient of humanism—would lead eventually to the triumph of the lowest common denominator. Many early observers of American democracy, too, worried about the possibility that it would turn into a "mobocracy." But we have ways of preventing that scenario: using the underlying principles of religion and secular education to promote humanism and thus democracy as well. Indeed, my proposed extension of humanist psychology—using the entelechial process as its matrix—should facilitate the spread of democracy on a secular basis to all societies, bringing about the eventual unity of humankind.

Everyone knows that dictators and terrorists exploit organized religion for their own purposes. The fact is that religion, like so many other valuable things, has two sides: a light one and a dark one. The light one fosters the entelechial process. I call that *humanist spirituality*. The dark side does not. I call that *axiopathy* to denote pathological values: those that violate human nature by opposing the development of a humanist society. Axiopathy is the use of religion, in other words, for nefarious purposes. More specifically, axiopathy does so to support oppressive regimes, notably the totalitarian ones of recent history.

Axiopathy is not confined to any particular religion or society; any religion or society can become axiopathic in one way or another. Axiopathy is the chief nemesis of democracy and therefore of any incipient humanist society. It denies human nature, despite misleading statements to the contrary, and consequently represses the human spirit. In chapter 4, I will discuss a method of fighting axiopathy.

Charles Templeton, author of Farewell to God, was a successful evangelist. In fact, he worked closely with Billy Graham. But then he lost his faith and gave up his vocation and religion. What made him abandon Christianity? He no longer believed in the literal truth of Noah's ark; he could not figure out how anyone could have built an ark with enough room for a pair of every species.[11]

But this is not the way that religion works. Most preachers use allegories in order to move their audiences. Without allegories, they would have to rely entirely on abstractions. Christianity and Judaism, at any rate, are not about engineering. They are about experiencing the sacred, as interpreted and expressed by

3

theologians, philosophers, painters, poets, or composers, and re-creating the world with that in mind, guided by priests and prophets at first but eventually by philosophers or ethicists as well. Religion is in the business of making life meaningful by helping people to discern order (the sacred) in the midst of what would otherwise be chaos (the profane).

As a humanist, I believe that only one thing matters: not the surface message of a biblical story but its underlying meaning—its possible influence in creating a humanist society. Obviously Templeton did not make that distinction.[12] From my point of view, we should evaluate religious ideas only by what effects they have on people. To the extent that allegorical interpretations promote health and prosperity, they are legitimate; to the extent that they do not, they are illegitimate. In other words, those that promote the entelechial process are good; those that do not are bad. Interpretation, in short, is everything.

Who should have the authority to interpret religious texts? From my perspective as a humanist, the answer is simple: anyone, whether religious or not, who understands the entelechial process and uses empirical evidence to evaluate the usefulness of a text in connection with it. If we assume that God created people as divine images, then we must assume something else in addition: The only correct interpretations are those that lead to the highest degree of self-actualization for the greatest number of those divine images. Any other interpretation must be not only false but also blasphemous.

No one in any healthy society would allow innocent people to be harmed by those who claim to be doing the will of God. Similarly, no one in a humanist society would encourage anyone to interpret scripture in a way that leads people to reject either the entelechial process or democracy.

Truth does not mean in religion what it means in the natural sciences. As a humanist, I believe that the function of religion is to convey humanist values in line with the entelechial process. But I believe also that religion is tautological and not empirical. Religious truths are stated as axioms or first principles, not as hypotheses to be verified or falsified (although we can indeed verify or falsify them, as humanists or moralists, in connection with their effect or likely effect on people).

Ideally, for a humanist, religious truth is whatever promotes a humanist society. This makes it possible for humanists to evaluate every religion from the outside and according to an objective standard, albeit a reductive one: how well it guides human nature toward its highest destiny.

The functions of science, on the other hand, are to study nature—including human nature—and to use the knowledge gained as a way of attaining human purposes. Scientists rely on empirical evidence, which means that old truths are continually being replaced by newer ones. I would say, therefore, that religious and scientific truths play different but synergistic roles in encouraging healthy behavior for both individuals and societies.

Religion defines relations not only between the human and nonhuman or superhuman, but also between the individual and the community. In that context, it defines the meaning of life, among many other things. That definition is not arbitrary, from a humanist perspective, if it acknowledges the entelechial process and therefore promotes a humanist society. Here is how science and religion work together: science supplies information about the conditions of daily life, and religion defines good and evil in connection with those conditions. Together, they allow people to maximize the good and minimize the evil. As for democracy, it is useful to the extent that it allows both science and religion the freedom to function effectively.

Consequently, human destiny depends on what religion pronounces as good or evil. To the extent that religion cares more about divine nature than human nature, of course, the result is likely to be axiopathy and therefore the destruction of democracy.

As the source of values, or a belief system, the axioma complex (minor constant A1, which I will discuss in appendix B) influences law. The axiomatic force explains why people of the same religion generally follow more or less the same path in social intercourse; they have the same values. People of different religions generally clash with each other; they have conflicting values.[13]

The axioma complex is what unifies and characterizes a whole society at any time and place. The axiomatic force could be what binds all Americans, despite their varied ancestry, into one people. And the same force binds all Israelis, despite their varied ancestry, into a people that is united enough to defeat much bigger enemies. By the same token, of course, this axiomatic force can bind people together in totalitarian societies. Among the most notorious of these were Nazi Germany and Soviet Russia.

Thus the axioma complex would be the primary and essential factor in the creation of a humanist society as well as in the eventual elimination of antihumanist ones.

All people have free will, and their values are individual ones. (For more on that, see minor constant A2 in appendix A.) So the axiomatic force's power does not mean that every individual within society must approve of humanist values or be bound by them. But every individual would have to take them into account while living within a humanist society. The axioma complex consists of society's religious and political values, after all, which determine the shape of that society. And the message from religion is the primary one in determining whether humanism and democracy can thrive.

If a humanist axioma complex encourages people to express the best that is in them, an antihumanist one encourages them to express the worst that is in them. It is due to the axiomatic force that democracies often produce benevolent leaders and dictatorships malevolent ones. The leaders of any country, whatever its belief system, exert a telling influence on people to conform. The axiomatic force explains why most immigrants from totalitarian countries to democratic ones such as the United States assimilate readily.[14]

Because humanism is based on human nature, it could become a habit that dictatorships would find hard to compete with or combat. My purpose in this book is to show what those humanist values are and how to cultivate and even spread them around the world on a secular basis.

Chapter 2

RELIGION AND HUMANISM

As a humanist, I believe that only one thing is constant and thus suitable as the measure of all things: the entelechial process that makes self-actualization possible. To evaluate any religion, therefore, we must ask how it affects that process and measure its effects on society. A society that is both humanist and democratic—these are closely related but not identical[15]—would allow the highest number of people to achieve self-actualization.

Scholars in the field of religious studies, as in every other field, disagree about many things. They lack enough evidence from the very remote past to do more than speculate about the origin of religion. Nonetheless, even speculation can be based on common sense and probability rather than fantasy. As far as scholars can tell from Paleolithic burial sites, the origin of religion probably coincided with the origin of *Homo sapiens*. Religion functions on at least two levels, the personal and the communal, so I need to say something about each before proceeding.

Whatever else personal religion does—and it does many things—it probably originated historically (and continues to originate existentially in the life cycle of every person) with the sense of wonder.[16] This is always a characteristic of children, but it is no less a characteristic of artists and scientists and other adults who continue to experience life as a voyage of discovery. Religious people, including many scientists, experience the cosmos not only as something mysterious and awesome but also as something beautiful and joyful and even "alive" in some sense. It calls out to them, and they reach out in response to be part of it. This experience of integration within or participation in the cosmos, the sine qua non of religion, is known in the West as *holiness* or *the sacred*, and in the East as *enlightenment*.

As for communal religion—usually known as *organized religion*—it probably originated with culture and therefore, once again, with *Homo sapiens*. Religion in this sense functions, apart from anything else, as every society's organizing principle. More specifically, it functions as the symbol system that allows every society to create order out of chaos, provide a coherent rationale for every institution, and thereby confer meaning and purpose on daily life. Clearly, no society would be possible without culture, and no culture without organized religion or some secular equivalent, such as a political ideology.[17]

Until very recently, however, organized religion was not an autonomous institution in its own right. That is why no word for religion existed in the early stages of many languages—including biblical Hebrew! Every institution—social, economic, political, artistic, and so on—was saturated with religious meanings that linked all of them into a coherent whole. It was only with the advent of modernity during the Renaissance that Western culture fragmented into autonomous and often conflicting institutions, including one called "religion." More recently, religion itself has fragmented further into liberal, conservative, fundamentalist, and other factions.

Personal religion and organized religion function together, because every society consists of persons who are nevertheless parts of society. The two overlap for another reason too: because many organized religions are elaborations of insights gained from the personal religious experiences of founders such as Jesus, Muhammad, and the Buddha.[18]

Because my point in this chapter is primarily about organized religion, I will say no more here about personal religion. The primary function of organized religion has always been to make either holiness or enlightenment—in humanist parlance, self-actualization—accessible to as many people as possible, not only in the present but also in the future. In other words, organized religion transmits insights, in the form of traditional lore, from one generation to the next. Otherwise, these insights would disappear very quickly and leave society with the task of having to reinvent the wheel over and over again.

Among those insights—but by no means the only ones—are ethical insights. Some religions focus more heavily or more explicitly than others on ethics.[19] But it would be a serious mistake to assume that any religion is reducible to a moral code—or in fact to anything other than the experience of either holiness or enlightenment. Moral codes are all derived in one way or another—as are doctrines, rituals, the arts, and so on—from that primary religious experience.

From a strictly humanist perspective, that primary religious experience is irrelevant. Humanists are interested only in religious moral codes, because these are the only religious productions that can be translated easily into secular terms and used to support the entelechial process and build a humanist society.

I have already discussed organized religion in connection with the axioma complex—that is, the religious or political worldview. (I discuss this more fully in appendix B.) This is the primary source of common values and therefore fosters either humanism and democracy or antihumanism and autocracy.

As for measuring the effects of religion, the standard is how well it serves the entelechial process, how effectively it fosters self-actualization, and therefore how successfully it creates or maintains a humanist society. The method is empirical, because it relies on evidence from the social sciences. From this point of view, it is legitimate to evaluate religions from the outside.[20] From my perspective as an outsider, I see that not all religions have been equally successful in supporting both humanism and democracy.[21] I turn now, therefore, to the question of which religions have been most and least successful.

Before proceeding, however, I must add one important caveat. Every one of the world religions is capable of supporting a humanist society. Every religion originated as or evolved into a way of life that fulfills fundamental human needs. Not one of these religions, in other words, is inherently incapable of doing so. To the extent that religions fail to support humanist societies—and all of them do fail to some extent, because there is no such thing as perfection in a finite world—we must look for explanations in particular historical contexts.

At present, only two forms of Western religion support humanism and therefore democracy. I refer to Christianity and Judaism.

Historical circumstances have allowed them to evolve a common worldview that, I believe, is a humanist one in religious clothing.

Since Vatican II, Catholicism has explicitly and consistently endorsed democracy (along with freedom of religion). But the most important link between democracy and religion involves Protestantism, because Protestantism, though inadvertently, made modernity possible in the first place and therefore democracy as well. Although Protestants trace their spiritual lineage back to biblical Judaism, Protestantism is significantly different from both biblical and rabbinic Judaism. And this difference—an intense focus on the individual—is precisely what led, indirectly, to the rise of modern democracies.

Both Judaism, whether biblical or rabbinic, and other forms of Christianity have embedded the individual within a holy community: the children of Israel, the church, the communion of saints (which links the living with the dead), and so on. From the very beginning, though, Protestants rejected that point of view and therefore made a radical break with the past. Every Protestant stands utterly alone before God and is theologically accountable to no one but God. Protestant denominations exist in order to facilitate encounters between the individual and God. They do not mediate salvation through the administration of sacraments, the intervention of saints, and so on. As institutions, of course, they must have structures that are based on function and authority. Some Protestant denominations even call their leaders "bishops" (and are Catholic in some other ways too). But the unique genius of Protestantism is its assertion of strictly personal responsibility for salvation. No matter what others in the community say or do, each individual must either personally accept the gift of salvation or personally reject it.

It is not hard to see what effect that would have on individuals and societies when translated into secular terms. The basic premise of democracy is that all citizens must take personal responsibility for making choices that affect themselves and society as a whole.[22] And those choices sometimes involve a high degree of personal risk.

The early Protestants did not set out to create modern and secular democracies, let alone to embrace the humanist virtue of tolerance. In fact, they set out to create theocracies based openly on intolerance. The colony in Massachusetts Bay, for instance, was hardly a model of tolerance or any other humanist virtue; on the contrary, it excluded everyone who failed to uphold Puritan orthodoxy. But a century later, when philosophers and revolutionaries were rethinking society in secular terms, Protestant habits of thought were still prevalent.[23] True, the new republic would separate church and state. The churches themselves insisted on this; the goal was not so much to protect the state from interference by the churches, but to protect the churches from interference by the state. Moreover, the new republic would be a democracy. But both secularity and democracy, in the eighteenth century, could rely on a largely Protestant civil society that had been trained for generations to value individualism and the civic responsibilities that individualism implied.[24]

It is surely no accident that all Protestant countries (or at least nominally Protestant ones) are democracies. Nor is it an accident that most democracies are Protestant (or at least nominally

Protestant). The most powerful democracy at the moment is clearly the United States of America, which demonstrates to my mind the legacy of Protestantism—which I consider a religious equivalent of humanism. In my opinion, therefore, the American system is an ideal model for world federalism.

I have less to say about liberal forms of Judaism, because these originated at least partly as attempts to imitate liberal forms of Protestantism. Unlike the Protestant Reformation in general or even the Reformed (Calvinist) churches in particular, Reform Judaism was not an attempt to recreate ancient religion in some pure form. On the contrary, it was an attempt to replace ancient religion with modern and secularized religion (the result of which, Reform Judaism, resembled modern and secularized Protestantism). They winnowed out whatever features of ancient Judaism could not advance the cause of integrating Jews into modern and secular European societies. Two other Jewish denominations, the Conservatives and the Reconstructionists, have done the same thing (although the latter has gone even further than Reform).

The point here is that nothing in traditional Judaism prepared the way even indirectly for democracy. Liberal forms of Judaism are now as compatible with democracy as liberal forms of Protestantism (and, as I will show, at least one other form of Christianity).

All religions contain some features that, when translated into secular terms, can support democracy. By the same token, all contain some features that, whether translated into secular terms or not, can support tyranny. It all depends on how people interpret their own sources. The fate of every religion, therefore, is in the hands of its interpreters. My approach makes it possible for interpreters to find the humanist traces in their religions and to establish these in connection with likely material and political benefits to their societies.

Consider the case of Japan during the American occupation that followed World War II. Japan had been a military dictatorship, one that was supported by a nationalistic interpretation of Shinto religion. But its new Japanese constitution was based directly on that of the United States and therefore indirectly on liberal Protestantism. In other words, from my point of view, it was based on humanism. This fact, along with others, has turned Japan into a successful democracy. Consider India too. Its new and secular constitution, influenced by British and American traditions, has curbed the antihumanist and antidemocratic caste system and other Hindu traditions that crept in over thousands of years and prevented social or economic change.[25]

Now, think about traditional religions that support humanism but might or might not support democracy. Think, for instance, of biblical and rabbinic forms of Judaism. Both have promoted what I would consider humanist virtues, ones that foster self-actualization. And neither has produced totalitarian regimes.[26] But the biblical kings—at least the ones that got good reviews in Scripture—created theocracies, not democracies.[27] Between AD 70 and 1948, moreover, Jews had no state at all. In other words, they lacked the political power to produce either democratic or totalitarian regimes. An argument from absence proves nothing. We have no way of knowing how Jews would have governed themselves if they had been able to maintain or create a state of their own during those twenty centuries.

Biblical Judaism and rabbinic Judaism have fostered humanist virtues such as justice and compassion. Whether they encourage these virtues in connection with those who live outside the Jewish community, however, is another matter—but an important one in any book on humanism and democracy in a "pluralistic" society, which is what most democracies now are.[28]

Even the Bible is ambiguous in this respect. "Love your neighbor," says the Book of Leviticus.[29] But precisely who is a neighbor? A fellow Israelite? A Canaanite? The Book of Ruth is famous for its inclusivity—that is, its welcoming approach toward non-Jews or at least toward those who, like Ruth herself, convert to Judaism.[30] By implication, they welcome even some non-Jewish ideas; the latter have heavily influenced Judaism during many stages of its development. The Book of Ezra, on the other hand, is almost as famous for its exclusivity—its indifference or hostility toward non-Jews (including the foreign wives and children of Jews returning from exile[31]) and by implication toward non-Jewish ideas as well, sometimes due to conflict with Jewish ones and sometimes merely for the sake of rejecting anything foreign.

This conflict is inherent in every society, of course, because there can be no such thing as a society unless it clearly distinguishes between insiders and outsiders, the familiar and the foreign. But it has been among the most enduring conflicts in Jewish societies, both biblical (which established a new identity for people who had left their former communities to found a new one) and rabbinic (which found ways for Jews to live as separate communities within non-Jewish and sometimes hostile societies). Modern

Jewish theologians and philosophers refer to this as the conflict between *universalism* (inclusivity, openness to the larger world) and *particularism* (exclusivity, withdrawal from the larger world).[32] Only Reform Judaism has defined itself explicitly in universalist terms, although even Reform Judaism has begun to reassert traditional particularism in the forms of Jewish ethnocentrism and nationalism.

In theory, then, it is true that traditional Judaism has a mission in the larger world: Jews will become what Isaiah calls a "light to the nations."[33] In practice, traditional Jews have usually ignored passages of that kind, interpreting them as idealistic references to some remote messianic age. They have often remained indifferent to other "nations," therefore, including their non-Jewish neighbors within the larger society—and even to their nontraditional Jewish neighbors in some cases.

This contradiction looks less formidable when you consider modern Jewish history. Since the nineteenth century, Jews have flocked to liberal and even revolutionary movements—some of which, though not all, could be considered humanist movements. They have been liberal and therefore, almost by definition, highly secularized Jews. Traditional—that is, religious—Jews have been appalled by most of those movements. They see no connection between those movements and Judaism. They do appreciate the religious tolerance that allows Jews in democratic countries to live and worship as they please, but they are not notably tolerant themselves. This is what the Israelis have learned from bitter conflicts between religious and secular political factions.

The humanist virtue of tolerance is not a traditional Jewish virtue, although it has become a modern Jewish virtue, because it was never a biblical virtue. Few biblical motifs are more common, in fact, than the ancient Israelite contempt for almost every neighboring society. Canaanites, Philistines, Egyptians, Babylonians, Assyrians—all are denounced over and over again. Some of those societies are denounced as current or former enemies, so some degree of hostility must have been almost inevitable. But King Saul's genocidal attack on the Amalekites, though motivated by revenge for an earlier genocidal attack, should be more than a little unsettling to humanists—not only because the biblical authors were clearly proud of it but also because they attributed its instigation to God[34] (who drives Saul from the throne for disobeying the command to kill every last Amalekite).[35] The biblical authors denounce other neighboring societies merely for worshipping alien gods—and worse, idols of alien gods.[36] Scripture does refer to a few good non-Israelites—the pharaoh who rewards Joseph; Ruth, the Moabite, who converts to the Israelite religion and becomes an ancestor of King David; the hapless citizens of Assur who heed the warning of Jonah and are thus saved from divine wrath; and Cyrus, the king of Persia, who releases the Israelites from exile. But these references are rare exceptions and usually apply to individuals rather than whole societies. The best that can be said of non-Israelites in the Bible, generally speaking, is vaguely foretold by the prophets: these other societies will eventually convert to the true religion of Israel.[37]

There are connections between some revolutionary movements and Judaism, actually, but not ones that all secular Jews would like to acknowledge. Marxism, for instance, is in many ways a secular version of biblical Judaism, which explains at least partly why so many Jews became Marxists and some remained Marxists, even when it became clear that Marxist ideology supported dictators such as Stalin. Like biblical Judaism, Marxism is based on a particular notion of history, one that philosophers call *dualistic*. For both, history is essentially a titanic conflict: good versus evil, the bourgeoisie versus the proletariat, polytheists versus monotheists, the "children of light" versus the "children of darkness," or simply us versus them. For both, history will come to an end with a final and spectacular victory of us over them. And for both, that will mean a utopian future: returning to paradise or Eden for Jews and establishing a "classless society" or a "dictatorship of the proletariat" for Marxists.

Why have secular Jews found these modern movements so attractive? Not because of anything in their religion, which they have rejected in any case, but because of their political situation. In the late eighteenth century and the early nineteenth, liberal and revolutionary movements were the only ones that allowed Jews to join. They promised to bring Jews out of their ghettoes and into mainstream society. It was the Enlightenment that convinced French and other philosophers of the eighteenth and early nineteenth centuries to argue for the political emancipation of Jews—that is, giving them full citizenship.

One way to legitimate their emancipation was for Jews to become like all other citizens except in the private realm of religion. Another way was for Jews to oppose repressive regimes by taking up arms with their non-Jewish counterparts—or, at the very least, to vote for liberal parties. Even though most modern (secular) Jews embrace humanism, in short, the reason has very little to do with Judaism.

Some religions currently make it possible for their followers to switch back and forth easily between democracy and autocracy.

They have come to contain within themselves, often at the cost of conflict, what I consider both humanist and antihumanist features. Either can be switched on or off depending on circumstances.

First, consider Catholicism. Ancient Judaism gave birth to Christianity—I refer here to what would eventually become Catholicism, as distinct from either Protestantism or Eastern Orthodoxy—and that Christianity presumably inherited any humanist values that Judaism had fostered. But if we use the metaphor of birth, we should do so consistently. In that case, we would have to say that Christianity, like all children, had not one but two parents. The other parent, of course, was Rome—that is, Greco-Roman civilization.

The latter influenced Christianity at a very early stage. Paul's letters, the earliest stratum of the New Testament, were written in the first century. These are saturated with both Jewish theological thinking and Greek philosophical thinking (but not, unfortunately, the kind of philosophical thinking that had supported the Athenian experiment with democracy). Long before Christianity became Rome's state religion, it had absorbed Rome's intellectual and artistic traditions.

Christianity reached a milestone in the fourth century when Constantine made it Rome's state religion. For the first time, the church had the power of a state behind it. That power grew, ironically, as the state itself crumbled. In effect, the church replaced the state; otherwise anarchy would have replaced empire. Christianity was no longer the religion of a small and sometimes persecuted community, but the only guarantor of public order. At its disposal were not only the imperial bureaucracy and the imperial courts of law, but also, eventually, the imperial armies.

In a way, the church's power was a blessing. It maintained whatever was left of a brilliant civilization, including the rule of law. In another way, though, the church's power was a curse. But that did not become evident to everyone before the late Middle Ages.

After the fall of Rome, the church reorganized itself, by necessity, as a government. Not only did it have to settle theological disputes, administer parish churches, translate or copy ancient manuscripts, and care for the poor, it now had also to perform the tasks that every government must perform: maintaining public order and the rule of law, encouraging trade and commerce, establishing political alliances, defending the state from increasingly aggressive invaders, and so on.

For these new tasks, the New Testament provided very little advice. The earliest Christians had expected the immediate return of Jesus and his inauguration of the eternal kingdom of God. Once it became clear that this return would be delayed, they had to make practical plans for a new order: not only spiritual but social, economic, and political as well. For the most part, they relied on the laws and customs that were already in place throughout the Greco-Roman world. They modified some of these, however, with the new religion in mind.

During the early Middle Ages, they had to consider an additional factor. The new kingdoms—those of the Vandals, the Visigoths, the Teutonic peoples, and so on—adopted Christianity, but also maintained many of their own legal, political, social, and other traditions. As a result of these cultural encounters and many more, Christianity developed the ability to transform itself and adapt to new conditions. Over many centuries and in many places, it absorbed and accumulated traditions (often for political reasons) that did not necessarily fit easily with the earliest Christian ones. History is about change, after all, not stasis.

Despite its name, the Reformation amounted to a revolution. By the late Middle Ages, many people realized that the church had lost its way. Protestants accused the church not only of theological contamination by alien sources, making it "pagan," but also of moral corruption. Power corrupts, according to the old saying, and absolute power corrupts absolutely. No pope ever had absolute power, but most popes by this time had enough power to indulge themselves in gross corruption.

To restore the alleged purity of early Christianity, some Protestants were ready to reform the church's teachings, to destroy centuries of artistic treasures and, of course, to kill those who stood in their way. In response, their adversaries—now identifiable as Roman Catholics—launched the Counter-Reformation. They cleaned up the moral corruption, but the result did not add up to what humanists would consider a religion that fostered either personal self-actualization (except in the limited sense of spiritual self-actualization) or collective self-actualization (since democracy would not be reinvented, by secularized Protestants, for several centuries).

In our time, Catholicism has moved decisively away from its *triumphalism*. That word refers to the arrogant mentality that emerged as one result of the church's acquisition of imperial power in the fourth century and continued until the Second Vatican Council in the 1960s. Though by no means democratic itself,[38] the post-Vatican II church has explicitly endorsed democracy for the larger society—including the freedom of religion that goes with it—and denounced totalitarian regimes. In fact, it played a major role in destroying European communism. Though opposed to Marxist-based liberation theology, it has fervently supported the poor, especially in Latin America, and has denounced raw capitalism. Most telling of all, it has not only repented for persecuting other religious communities but also endorsed genuine dialogue with them—especially with Judaism.[39] This trend toward what I consider humanism rose to prominence with Vatican II,[40] but it had begun decades earlier. And though prompted historically by the rise of modernity and secularity, it relied ultimately on the restoration of ideas that had been present, though often ignored, since the early Christian period.

Both non-Catholics and disaffected Catholics like to attack the current Roman Catholic Church for its conservative policies on sex and the family. But these policies are deeply rooted in a way of thinking that is, even if you disagree with this or that policy, concerned with the good of society and uses evidence from the social sciences to back up, though not to prove, its point of view.

Consider the example of a country with Catholic traditions. France derives its antihumanist values from medieval Catholicism and its humanist ones from the Enlightenment. Not surprisingly, the French were ambivalent about democracy for a long time. During the nineteenth century, France became both a republic several times, a monarchy several times, and even an empire several times. Although France did not become a monarchy again during the twentieth century, it did develop a large colonial empire overseas. As for the Vichy regime, it, along with many of its citizens, collaborated with the Nazis during World War II.

After the liberation, France turned once again to democracy and with great enthusiasm. It has remained strongly democratic ever since, although it once supported the strongest Communist party in western Europe.

What if historical conditions once again promote French antihumanism? Now that the Roman Catholic Church has been transformed by Vatican II, it could become a humanist resource and therefore reinforce the secular Enlightenment. On the other hand, France, like every other country in western Europe, has become so thoroughly secular that few would take advantage of that resource.[41]

Hinduism is full of surprises due to its extreme complexity and lack of any central authority. It has long been ruled by empires, some Indian and others foreign, some benevolent and others brutal. The British established many of the institutions on which democracies rely—notably the civil service, courts of law, and schools—and trained Indians very carefully before leaving in 1947. Involvement in Mahatma Gandhi's Congress Party and observation of his negotiations with the British parliament taught many Indians about democratic government.

On the surface, it would seem that India had no democratic tradition until the British arrived. In fact, democracy was not completely new to India even before the Raj. Villages had always been run by locally elected councils (*panchayats*), for instance, although their democratic character was mitigated until 1882 by caste considerations. Their practical decisions on local matters have usually been just as important to villagers as the grand policies of imperial rulers far away. Moreover, Hinduism has produced unusually rich intellectual, spiritual, and artistic traditions.

Anyone who looks below the surface can find humanist values deeply embedded in the Upanishads and in later philosophical and theological traditions. As a result, Hindu India has eagerly and successfully embraced democracy.

Few Buddhist countries have been democracies, but Buddhism is just as compatible with democracy as any other religion is and more compatible than some are because of the priority that it gives to humanist virtues such as compassion and reason.[42] But history has been unkind to eastern and southeastern Asia.

Confucianism emerged in the context of an imperial bureaucracy. Although it could have supported democracy due to its respect for humanist virtues, strangely like Jewish ones,[43] China was taken over ruthlessly by another Western political system. The Communists, unlike the British, rejected democracy in principle.[44]

It would be unfair—and even perverse in view of the grassroots democratic movement that rose up in Tiananmen Square—to say that the Chinese have "chosen" communism, much less that anything in their tradition predisposed them to communism or any other form of tyranny. According to Chinese tradition, even emperors relied on the "mandate of heaven." This mandate could be withdrawn from brutal or incompetent emperors and sometimes was withdrawn. In that case, revolution was a legitimate response to misrule.

Until the twentieth century, Confucianism provided the stability of good government, instilled a respect for learning and the arts, and fostered civility in daily life. Even though China itself has tried to eradicate Confucianism, millions of Chinese in other countries and other parts of the world have maintained it (albeit in various combinations with Taoism and Buddhism) at the level of personal religion. To the extent that Confucianism has informed the traditional Chinese worldview, we must give it credit for modern democracies such as Taiwan and Singapore.

There is no such thing as an inherently axiopathic religion. All of the world religions can support humanist societies. But not all religious communities do so to the same extent, depending on historical circumstances. Some of them support political systems that have so far been hostile to democracy, though not necessarily to other aspects of humanism. In this category, I would include Islamic fundamentalists—which is to say, Islamic communities that have understood modernity as a threat and reacted against it with unreasonable and even extreme measures. Doing so has meant returning not to a golden age of purity, as the fundamentalists claim, but to a version of that golden age that has been severely distorted by frustration and rage.[45]

Islam, like Christianity, originated partly as a new version of Judaism. Unlike either Judaism or Christianity, though, Islam began almost immediately as a state. And not merely a state but a conquering state.

At first, the Islamic empire offered some conquered peoples—Jews and Christians as "peoples of the book"—religious freedom.[46] As non-Muslims, though, even they were subject to an extra tax and to various legal disabilities. Like all other premodern civilizations, early Islam insisted on the theological equality of all believers but knew nothing of social or political equality.[47] At various times and places, moreover, Islamic regimes persecuted both Jews and Christians.

As for Hindus and other conquered pagans, Islam ruled them with varying attitudes. Some Mughal emperors of India in the sixteenth and seventeenth centuries, notably Akbar, were not merely tolerant of other religions but fascinated to the point of bringing their leaders to their courts and engaging in religious dialogue with them. Dara Shukoh went even further and tried to invent a new religion that combined elements from many older ones. Aurangzeb, on the other hand, had no interest in any religion but Islam and treated Hindus with open contempt. His approach prevailed until British rule replaced Islamic rule. This explains, at least partly, the hostility between Hindus and Muslims in India that continues to this day. But that is not the whole story of Islam.

Early Islam was open to the wisdom of all conquered civilizations. Its philosophers translated Greek, Latin, Persian, and Chinese manuscripts. Using both ancient and foreign learning, they became innovators in fields such as mathematics, astronomy, and medicine. Muslim architects and painters and poets, too, gathered motifs from many traditions. Islamic cities were big, prosperous, safe, and lively. Long before European cities, Islamic ones had paved streets that were illuminated at night, fire brigades, libraries, and so on. By and large, they lived in peace and harmony with non-Muslims. Muslims, Christians, and Jews remember Baghdad in the east and Cordoba in the west as the venues of golden ages.

After a few centuries, though, Islam closed down; it stopped looking outward. Bernard Lewis and other scholars have asked what went wrong.[48] No single answer is adequate, although I should add here that this problem began long before the Europeans established colonies or mandates in Islamic countries. Whatever the reason, Islamic regimes—certainly the Ottomans—were succumbing to lassitude and even corruption by the eighteenth century.[49]

Nothing that I have said so far should be taken to mean that Islam prevents self-actualization, much less that it places no value on compassion, reason, and other humanist virtues. By the late nineteenth century, renewal movements had begun to develop in many Islamic countries. Some movements advocated religious reform; others advocated secular reform or nationalism. Some wanted to emulate Western notions of democracy; others wanted to develop distinctively Islamic versions of democracy.

So far, unfortunately, political problems have undermined these peaceful movements, fostered fundamentalism, allowed dictatorships, and even spawned terrorism. In this dreary context, readers should note that a growing number of Muslims do indeed acknowledge these problems. Not many Iraqis, for instance, were sorry to see the demise of Saddam Hussein's regime. Many Muslims blame the United States, in fact, for supporting dictatorial regimes in Arab countries. Muslims living in Western countries are finally speaking out against Islamic fundamentalism. Among them is Irshad Manji, who calls—at some risk to her own safety—for an Islamic reformation.[50]

As for fundamentalist religion in general, a cynical explanation would be that unscrupulous sociopaths favor it in order to gain control over a community, use that control to exploit people for personal gain (social, economic, or political), and then justify their own behavior and the submission of everyone else by quoting religious texts that were originally intended for very different purposes. There are people who do things like that. But much more is involved in most cases.

Fundamentalism is a surprisingly complex phenomenon and can be found in all three Western religious traditions—Judaism, Christianity,[51] and Islam—and even in some Eastern ones.[52] In fact, as Paul Nathanson and Katherine Young have argued, it can be found also in political ideologies, which function as secular religions.[53] Fundamentalism originates characteristically not in the fevered brains of sociopaths but in the real needs of people who are caught between two conflicting worldviews, one traditional and the other modern. (The self-consciousness of this reaction against modernity means that even the most conservative fundamentalist communities are different in one way from genuinely conservative, or traditional, ones.)

Some fundamentalists, such as Hamas, resort to violence against the larger society. Others withdraw from society instead, such as the ancient Essenes, the Hasidim, the Amish, and the Hutterites. Some fundamentalist leaders are opportunistic charlatans, like the televangelist Jim Bakker, but others sincerely believe in what they preach, like Billy Graham.

Some fundamentalist communities fail to satisfy basic human needs and do not survive either internal or external pressure. Others do satisfy basic human needs and endure or even grow from one generation to the next, like the Pentecostals. Some fundamentalist organizations are autocratic, as for example the Jonestown cult was, but others are democratic, like the Southern Baptists.

As a humanist, my problem is with fundamentalist groups such as Hamas that exploit rage and distort the underlying religion—in this case Islam, which opposes both suicide and murder for political purposes.

Distorted religions fail to foster democracy. Sometimes they actively foster dictatorship. Dictatorship, unlike fundamentalism, is always linked with tyranny.

Precisely which regimes should we classify as dictatorships? The answer is not as easy as you might imagine. Although the word "dictator" was used in ancient Rome for a magistrate who was appointed to handle an emergency, we associate it with modern tyrants such as Hitler, Mussolini, Stalin, Mao, Idi Amin, Pol Pot, and so on. My original inclination was to argue that all premodern states—that is, nondemocratic ones—were dictatorships and therefore not only antihumanist but also axiopathic. However, this argument would erase any significant difference between the truly horrendous regimes of the twentieth century and countless ordinary ones throughout history. On purely moral grounds, that kind of leveling—all political leaders before George Washington were the moral equivalents of Nazis—would be facile, to say the least.[54] Besides, any objective look at history reveals a much more complicated picture.

In a way, the history of dictatorship can be traced back to the rise of early states. First, though, some background information. Before the Agricultural (or Neolithic) Revolution, there were no states. People lived in small bands of hunters and gatherers. As far as we can tell by analogies with present-day hunting-and-gathering societies, only two tasks were specialized: childbirth for women and hunting for men, although women supplemented resources by gathering plants. In communities that relied on fishing rather than hunting, women probably did that as well.

Because most tasks could be done by anyone, and because even the particular risks for both men and women were roughly equal—dying in childbirth or being killed by animals—these societies were egalitarian. And because they probably made decisions by consensus, their societies could be described as democracies, though not, of course, representative democracies that relied on elaborate parliamentary institutions.

Everything changed with the development of agriculture. The new technology made it possible for people to produce their own food, and much more of it than ever before. This gave rise to urbanization, professional specialization, and social stratification. Agriculture itself required a high degree of both specialization and organization. While some people were plowing the fields, others were engaged in the many closely related tasks: smelting iron for the plows, designing and building irrigation canals, and designing and building granaries or temples (which served not only as places of worship but also as markets and distribution centers). Those specializations gave rise in turn to many others: designing and building ships to transport food from one place to another, trading local products for the products of other communities, writing down local myths (which often conveyed information not only about the gods but also about the environment), keeping records of all commercial transactions, building cities for rapidly expanding populations, establishing and enforcing legal codes, and so on. Someone had to administer all these activities and coordinate them. Everyone depended on that person—first a clan elder, then a tribal chief, and then a king—who, in turn, depended on distinct classes of educated and trained scribes, magistrates, soldiers, merchants, traders, priests, farmers, and so forth.

Some kings turned out to be worthy; they presided over prosperous communities and either established or maintained laws based on fairness. Others turned out to be unworthy. They presided over poverty-ridden or strife-ridden communities, ignored the law, and so forth. The Bible records both kinds, not only in connection with Egypt and other countries but also, according to the prophets, in connection with both Israel and Judah.

The earliest chiefs and kings were ruthless. They had to disregard the egalitarian traditions of hunting-and-gathering societies, not to mention common decency, in order to assume power. Not surprisingly, many of them decided that no laws or even customs applied to them. They typically captured and raped hundreds of wives, killed thousands of men to suit whims, and indulged themselves in every luxury available to them. These early heads of state, not later kings, were the real prototypes of modern dictators. These rulers had absolute power, or as close to absolute power as mortals can get. Of greater interest here, though, is the profound reaction that their excesses generated.

This reaction amounted to the rise of much more complex religious systems. By the time that those early states developed into large-scale civilizations, after many hundreds of years, people had begun to think carefully and systematically about the pervasive unhappiness and pessimism that megalomaniacal rulers fostered. People had begun to think about the suffering of innocent people, in other words, along with the need for universal standards of justice and the ideal of compassion. Eventually, most kings came to rule—in practice though not always in theory—within the larger ethical and legal contexts of new theologies or philosophies, those we now call the "world religions."

We are all familiar with the divinely ordained rules that were supposed to guide ancient Israelite kings, who came along rather late in the history of state formation. God required them to show compassion for the poor, the widow, the orphan, and so on. But very similar rules guided other kings, and not only in the ancient Near East. The kings of Mesopotamian city-states and later empires were the stewards of divine estates, but the same basic principles—the ones that constrained Israelite kings—applied to them as well.

In theory, the Egyptian pharaoh was not a steward but a divine incarnation. In practice, though, the same constraints applied to him. Every pharaoh was expected to maintain truth and justice (*ma'at*), and therefore prosperity, for the entire nation according to a paradigm that the gods had established at creation. Indeed, that was his raison d'être; any pharaoh who failed to maintain it had no legitimacy and was likely to be overthrown. Being overthrown meant not merely losing power but being erased, literally, from all historical records and therefore denied immortality. Any pharaoh might be better or worse than most, but all were measured by a single divinely ordained standard—one that evolved considerably over the millennia of Egyptian history.[55]

The rise of very early states was accompanied by the origin of war. Hunting-and-gathering groups were always on the move. While searching for new hunting grounds, they often met other groups doing the same thing. But the territory could seldom support more than one group at a time. An obvious solution was

33

simply for the two groups to move in opposite directions. Before the earliest states emerged, there would have been no point in one group raiding the other, because neither had stored food or any significant stock of implements (all of which would have been too heavy for any group to carry along on its perpetual travels).[56]

Agricultural societies were settled, on the other hand. They did keep stores of surplus food, because agriculture depended on the weather, which was somewhat unpredictable. They also possessed large holdings of implements and other products. This made them ideal targets for raiders from other communities—especially those in search of more fertile land, better access to water, and sometimes slaves as well.

Pastoral societies, which wandered with their herds, also had property—animals—that could be raided. Those societies were even more given to raiding than agricultural ones, in fact, because their travels enabled them to steal the property of both settled communities and other nomadic ones. War, in short, became a potentially profitable enterprise, not only for the king and his entourage but also—especially in connection with new or better land—for the entire community.

Very few of these ancient societies liked war. The Greeks were unusual in this respect, partly because they were as pastoral as they were agricultural. But most were prepared to put up with it in the hope of winning better conditions. Despite its reputation in the Bible, Egypt seldom resorted to war during its first two thousand years. It was hardly ever attacked by outsiders except during the two interregnal periods, when public order collapsed, due to its geographical isolation by deserts.

Even though the Egyptians (especially in later times) expected their kings to display at least nominal martial prowess, they did not expect that of everyone. On the contrary, the ideal man valued learning, especially medicine, and justice. The ideal man was a family man, moreover. According to letters written on potsherds by workers on building projects, he enjoyed being in the company of his wife, playing with his children, and enjoying the beauty of his garden. This was not a martial, or "heroic," society.

Not one of these ancient kingdoms resembled a modern democracy, although many allowed democratic processes at the local level. The Greeks and Romans did develop democracies of a kind, but only a tiny and elite segment of each society could vote or even speak out on public affairs. That segment excluded women in Greece and to some extent also in Rome.[57] Both, moreover, were slave societies.[58] It is worth remembering, however, that the Southern Confederacy was both a slave society *and* a democratic one.[59]

In any case, it would be very ungenerous to condemn ancient societies for lacking both the wisdom that comes from hindsight and the bureaucratic machinery of modern times. It is true that not even the most impassioned archaeologist would want to recreate ancient Babylonian or Chinese society in the modern world. And very few Jews or Christians, if any, would want to recreate ancient Israelite society; the Bible recognizes that this society was far from ideal even by its own standards. Fascinating and admirable though some of those societies were in some ways, they could not satisfy the needs of modern people, certainly not those of us who value democracy (let alone high technology).

But we should be able to look at many of these societies realistically and even sympathetically as the products of people very much like ourselves who lived in conditions that we would find intolerably harsh. Even royal heirs often died in early childhood. Even kings had to work and risk being killed in battle. People could do almost nothing to avoid plagues, although the Egyptians found ways of curing many diseases and avoiding famines. The wonder is not that they had less freedom than we do but that they had any at all.

Within the context of tradition and law, some rulers took advantage of their power to exploit their subjects; they were axiopaths. Others used their power to rule wisely; they were protohumanists.

Not much about the state changed until modern times and the rise of rationalistic, nationalistic, or other revolutionary ideologies—although the rise of democracy actually began earlier, in medieval England, with the Magna Carta.[60] The same basic principles that applied to the kings of Israel and Egypt applied also to European and other kings until very recently, when some of them were replaced by dictators, who, like the earliest chiefs, were guided by nothing more than personal whim. Some monarchs tried to use their power for purely selfish purposes, and others did not.

Henry VIII of England set out to be a Renaissance prince. In his youth, he was a renowned humanist, as people understood that word in the sixteenth century: charming, highly educated, articulate in both theology and philosophy, and talented as a composer of music. Later on, though, his interests focused on political intrigue. He became arrogant and even brutal. Despite his own theological misgivings, Henry deliberately fostered

36

Protestantism (which had already produced a growing community in England) in order to legitimate his assertion of supreme power over the church in England and therefore to legitimate his succession of divorces, murders, and remarriages. Ostensibly, these resulted from his concern for providing an heir to the throne and therefore political stability for England. Even at the time, though, it was clear to many people that his main concern was to satisfy his own vanity. He did very little for England.

It was his daughter, Elizabeth, who presided over an English golden age. She was certainly no democrat, wielding much more power than any modern president or prime minister, but she was hardly a dictator in anything like either the very ancient sense of that word or the modern.

Two generations later, Charles I claimed the "divine right" of kingship. What he meant, however, was the divine right to reign, not a divine right to rule or behave in any way he pleased. By virtue merely of claiming a divine right, Charles acknowledged a divine obligation: to rule in accordance with God's will as revealed in Christianity (specifically Protestantism in this case). And when he failed to maintain the legitimacy even of his reign, Charles was deposed, tried in court, and executed.

I have pointed out a link between the dictators of very ancient times, those of Neolithic societies, and those of very recent times. In both settings, rulers were—pardon the modern and somewhat anachronistic terminology—antihumanist and antidemocratic. Consider some modern ones.

Saddam Hussein never showed the slightest interest in Islam—not even the Sunni Islam of his power base. Stalin and his many clones in eastern Europe never showed the slightest interest in

Christianity (except, of course, when it came to persecuting Christians)—not even in the Orthodox Christianity of their populations. Neither have their peers in Latin America, on the left or the right, shown the slightest interest in Catholicism (except for murdering nuns, priests, and even an archbishop). And Hitler had nothing but contempt for Christianity, which he considered not only a form of Judaism but also a serious rival to both his own version of ancient Teutonic religion and his pseudoreligion of National Socialism.

The same variety has been true in societies once based on Eastern religions. Pol Pot never showed the slightest interest in Buddhism. As for Mao, he never showed the slightest interest in Confucianism, Taoism, or Buddhism; on the contrary, he tried to wipe out every trace of them.

Hirohito (or at least those who acted in his name), on the other hand, deliberately fostered Shinto. As the traditional Japanese religion, Shinto not only venerated the local spirits but also glorified the imperial lineage in a way that fostered intense nationalism and therefore supported militarism.

This brings me to what could be considered a paradox. Some of these modern dictatorships, notably those of the Communists and Nazis, produced and venerated their own scriptures, invented their own rituals, and imitated religion in other ways to glorify their secular regimes. It might be most helpful to follow Nathanson and Young, who have argued that political ideologies are really "secular religions."[61] As they point out, these ideologies function in almost every way as religions, except for making the sacred accessible.

We often think of political ideologies in connection with widespread poverty and high birthrates. But even at the height of a worldwide depression, Nazi Germany had both a high standard of living and a high birthrate. The Soviet Union had both a low standard of living (by Western standards) and a low birthrate (along with a high abortion rate). Communist China had both a low standard of living and, by law, a low birthrate.

But some features characterize all of these societies: dictatorship accompanied by pervasive corruption and a general lack of respect for the individual. For humanists, these add up to denial of the entelechial process.

As I have said, though, traditional religions give me hope. I find comfort as a humanist in the fact that even those that have seemingly succumbed to axiopathy have roots that are not at all axiopathic and could still foster both humanism and democracy. Axiopathic societies are bound to collapse, in any case, because they do not and cannot satisfy basic human needs.

Chapter 3

SCIENCE AND DEMOCRACY

Just as we need traffic laws to drive safely, we need laws of conduct to produce a humanist society. But first, we must know the laws that govern human nature. In other words, we must first know how the entelechial process actually works. Only then can we establish a firm foundation—a scientific foundation that relies on empirical evidence and hypotheses that are either verifiable or falsifiable—for both ethics and law in a humanist society.

As a humanist, I believe that science, not religion, must have the last word. The will of God as revealed in scripture might or might not agree with the evidence of science. But science can do more than verify or falsify religious doctrines. Its ultimate function in a humanist society would be to establish what would be best for the entelechial processes of as many people as possible—that is, what would work best for a humanist society in any circumstance. And if scientists make mistakes, as they do, then either they or later scientists can correct those mistakes. This is how science works.

With this in mind, I have developed a humanist code: the ethical and legal principles that would be necessary for any humanist society. Ideally, we could derive these principles directly from human nature. And we can do so now that we know how the entelechial process actually works.[62] My goal, then, is to transform both ethics and law into reliable sciences that are compatible with human nature.

The various world religions have already established many of these principles. The Universal Declaration of Human Rights, published by the United Nations in 1948, has added others. But we must accept even those rights on faith, as it were, because they are not based on scientific evidence about human nature. Like any religious text, but without even a coherent philosophical context, this document simply declares that this or that is a right, a duty, a truth. Whether religious or secular, documents of this kind are likely to be misunderstood or misused, and indeed have been historically.

What we need is an external standard by which to evaluate these principles. I refer once again to science. But I refer more specifically to the social sciences. Psychologists can tell us a great deal about the way people think and behave. So can sociologists and anthropologists. With their studies in mind, we can make sensible choices. Ways of thinking and behaving that are likely to prove beneficial to most people are morally good from this perspective and should therefore be encouraged legally. Ways of thinking or behaving that are unlikely to prove beneficial are immoral and should be illegal as well. As a humanist, I would define both ethics and law as social sciences that make it possible for us to build a humanist society.

In that case, we should test religious insights in the hope that many will prove useful and thus establish continuity with familiar traditions. We would have to discard those that do not prove useful. The validity of any principle lies not in its intrinsic truth or authority, much less on the intrinsic truth or authority of any religion, but on its likely contribution to building a humanist society and to opposing antihumanist regimes or movements. The humanist code is not a collection of doctrines, in other words, but a logical and deductive system that is based on knowledge of human nature—although it confirms many religious insights that our ancestors observed or intuited over many centuries of human experience. All of the world's religions have some humanist values.

One important task, therefore, is to translate these religions into secular terms and thus make them available to humanists and to society as a whole. Here, then, are the religious axioms that require translation.

> Axiom 1: God created the universe and continues to guide it in beneficial ways.

> Axiom 2: We are among God's most important creations; each of us bears the divine image and each is endowed with a unique entelechy. Human self-actualization is therefore also divine self-actualization.

> Axiom 3: God has granted everyone the right to self-actualization. This right may be limited only in the interest of someone else's right. In other words, society is more important than any of its members. This is the first principle of justice, or social humanism.

Axiom 4: As part of the divine plan, God requires us to do two things. First, we must establish social institutions—including governments—that lead to the self-actualization of as many people as possible. Second, we must oppose tyranny as a violation of self-actualization. In other words, God regards tyranny as the worst of all sins.

Axiom 5: Something innate and known only to God survives after death. God will keep faith with those who serve him in truth until the end of time.

And here are the secular theorems that emerge from those religious axioms, forming the humanist code.

Theorem 1: Humanist values are universal and thus suitable for everyone, no matter what they believe. Nature does not care if one believes that night is day or vice versa. Day is day and night is night. Humanist values are determined by human nature, not philosophical or religious beliefs.

Theorem 2: But to the extent that religious ideas are interpreted in ways that agree with scientific ideas about human nature, humanists can reconcile the two points of view.

Theorem 3: Religion and science work synergistically; each checks the other. Both would be essential in a humanist society.

Theorem 4: Humanists define axiopathy as any religious idea that favors tyranny. Furthermore, they use empirical evidence from the social sciences to reveal the likely extent of that tyranny and make laws to prevent it.

Theorem 5: Humanists acknowledge that religion nourishes people, which is why no civilization has ever been able to do without religion, even though some regimes have tried to replace it with their own political ideologies or "secular religions." Unlike science, religion relies on the congruence of doctrine with human nature. A humanist might believe in any religious doctrine, therefore, as long as it does not conflict with human nature.

Theorem 6: We do not know about the intrinsic truth of any religious claims, but we can know how they affect people by measuring them. Humanists have no problem with religious ideas if they affect people in ways that foster the entelechial process and therefore promote a humanist society.

Theorem 7: Religious ideas that affect people in ways that do not foster the entelechial process are axiopathic—crimes in the name of religion. Religion and science are both necessary functions of the entelechial process. The former tells us why we are here and what our mission is; the latter tells us how to achieve that mission by using natural laws. The former comes from a source higher than ourselves and is verified by empirical assessment of the conditions in which we live; the latter teaches us about the natural world, including the entelechial process. The former guides; the latter verifies.

If ethics were to become an empirical science based on human nature, it would eliminate disputes over different beliefs. Moral strength is the sine qua non of every society. Every society starts out by introducing some humanist values. These work well for a while until decline sets in; values become outdated, or they are violated by opportunistic rulers and ruling classes. In other words, humanism turns into antihumanism. We have no reason to assume on historical grounds that the fate of any democracy will be different, although my humanist belief is that it will. So far, every civilization has declined and fallen. But those civilizations were based on territory. Not all civilizations are based on territory—or at least not exclusively on territory.

Some minority communities—Jewish, Chinese, Indian—actually have a big historical advantage over any host society, because their destinies are not tied exclusively to territory; they are tied instead to several host societies. When one of those declines or is overrun, minority communities can easily continue to flourish among their own kind somewhere else.

While Jews were suffering persecution or being expelled from one place, for instance, they were flourishing in another place—and usually in many other places. What they lost in space (a state of their own), they gained in time (endurance).[63] Now that Jews have a state of their own, of course, Jewish history might take a different course. If most Jews were either to assimilate and disappear into the societies of non-Jewish countries or migrate to Israel, then Jewish civilization would be tied once again to territory—to the destiny of a state that, like all others, will eventually decline and fall for one reason or another.

My aim in this chapter has been to show how religion and science can cooperate in producing a society that is not only humanist but also democratic. I believe that the main purpose— the only purpose—of the latter is to foster the former.

Chapter 4

SOCIAL DEVOLUTION

The second law of thermodynamics states that everything in nature tends to run down. I suggest that the humanist equivalent would be a law of social devolution: all institutions tend toward either decline or tyranny unless guided by the humanist code.

The primary ingredient for any society is a humanist worldview, one that allows most people to achieve self-actualization and therefore to create the kind of dynamism that allows neither decline nor tyranny. Humanism would be for culture what oxygen is for the body.

Think of Persian civilization, which began with the humanist worldview of Zoroastrianism. A telling symptom of Persian decline was the failure of its armies to resist those of the Greeks. Persian soldiers abandoned the field of battle because they were not motivated to fight. On the contrary, they welcomed the Greeks and even joined them. They considered Alexander their liberator from tyranny at home.

Here is another and more pertinent example of the same thing. Islamic civilization began with a humanist worldview. Jews, Christians, and Zoroastrians welcomed the rule of Islam, some converting to Islam, because it promised to liberate them from tyranny. Eventually, though, Islam began a gradual decline and has so far not recovered. I referred to this problem in chapter 3 and would add here only that one reason was probably the accumulation of antihumanist values.

Like Western civilization, which went through several declines and rebirths, Islamic civilization might yet transform itself into something new. Mustafa Kemal Atatürk tried to modernize Turkey after its defeat in World War I, and was moderately successful, but at the cost of marginalizing Islam itself. He was followed by Reza Shah Pahlavi of Iran.

By that time, though, Muslims were getting ready to retaliate against modernization. They saw it, not without reason, as a new form of Western imperialism. They attacked the new shah, also not without reason, for being in league with Western oil interests. Eventually, they overthrew the monarchy and established an Islamic republic.

As a humanist, I would have to describe the ayatollah Khomeini, who took over, as axiopathic. But no evidence suggests that he was insincere. He truly believed that he was doing God's work by trading freedom for fundamentalism.

Every civilization is a complex and delicate mechanism. To defeat the law of social devolution, humanists must make clear to everyone how that law works. This leads me to an important practical question that all democracies must ask: how far should we take a good idea or follow a good policy before either modifying or abandoning it?

Physicians know what to do in analogous cases. They observe how actual patients respond to medications, as distinct from hypothetical patients, and then act accordingly. In other words, empirical evidence—not theory—dictates practice. The same would be true for humanists planning for the future of democratic societies. They would maintain ideas and policies as long as those ideas and policies keep working. Once they stop working, humanists would either modify or abandon them.

A good example is the preoccupation of American foreign policy with self-determination for all nations. Unfortunately, this noble idea works only for nations that are prepared by humanist values to establish and sustain democracies. After World War II, American diplomats began to pressure European countries to grant their colonies immediate independence, partly on the assumption that this would strengthen American influence in the new countries.

But most of these new countries were not ready for democracy. When the Europeans left, local bullies rushed in to fill the political void as dictators. In some ways, the people were worse off than they had been under colonial rule.

Humanists would have removed forms of tyranny such as apartheid immediately, then placed these countries under the care of an international organization until they were ready to establish democratic governments. Self-determination was a good idea, but it did not always work well in practice; it required modification to suit the circumstances.

Here is another example of a good idea that could get out of hand but has not in the United States. The First Amendment guarantees every American freedom of speech, but its legal interpreters have recognized that there is a limit to everything. No one has a right to scream "Fire!" in a crowded theater. Similarly, no one has a right to advocate illegal activities such as terrorism or to incite violence by spreading hatred against identifiable communities. (Slander is a protected form of speech, in a way, but the victims of slander have a right to sue for defamation.)

The general humanist principle here is that one's freedom should be protected unless it infringes on the freedom or rights of anyone else. We must always reject absolute freedom of speech. According to the law of social devolution, that would inevitably produce antihumanist conditions and lead to the demise of democracy.

Chapter 5

HUMANIST POLITICS

Many people think of democracy as a system of government that is based on periodic elections—which is to say, on how the majority votes. Even though that is indeed an essential feature of democracy, it is a secondary one. Primary, from a humanist point of view, would be human rights that are derived from nature and therefore verifiable by social scientists. These rights are, by definition, universal and recognized by law. This is what truly unites people and thus makes a majority vote meaningful.

Because laws are made only to benefit the people, the people must make sure by voting that legislators pass only useful laws. The purpose of democracy is to achieve a humanist society and that the mechanism for doing so is a *humanist structure*. I would define the latter two-dimensionally: humanist structure = humanist code:humanist politics. This equation means that a human society's structure is governed by the humanist code, which establishes the forms of humanist politics—the constitution, the divisions of governmental power, the electoral system, the bureaucracy, and so on—in order to make society as effective as possible.

Thus the most important part of democracy is a legal system that respects human nature and rights. Otherwise, any social system will sooner or later collapse. Nature is relentless when it comes to the violation of any of its laws, including those of society. Laws based on nature are the only mechanisms that can sustain democracy.

A democratic humanist society would therefore be both the most natural and the most effective venue for human existence. But it would not be a utopia. Utopias are not real, because they are not based on human nature. A humanist democracy would bring out the best in people. It would add nothing, but it would also subtract nothing. An antihumanist dictatorship, on the other hand, would bring out the worst in people. It would indeed subtract something: the security provided by rights.

In looking at the various dimensions of democracy, I find that two of them, the humanist society and the humanist code, are based on nature and therefore not subject to arbitrary change. But humanist political activities are subject to change, careful change, according to need. As a humanist, I want to produce the most effective but least expensive system of government. The latter can take many forms as long as it is guided by the humanist code and designed to bring about a humanist society.

American democracy is distinguished by over two centuries of (sometimes halting) progress toward humanism by expanding human rights. It has been able to overcome slavery and slavery's lengthy aftermath of racial segregation and violence. Most Americans now believe that all citizens should have equal rights. As a result, Americans enjoy a high level of self-actualization.

Though far from perfect, the United States is among the most fully humanist and democratic countries.

Canada, Israel, Japan, and many European countries have adopted the closely related parliamentary system. The least successful of them have incorporated proportional representation, which tends to allow too many warring parties and therefore leads to factionalism and paralysis. Proportional representation was very problematic in France and still is in Israel.

But humanists have not been active for very long in politics, about two centuries. In the future, we will have to reject the one-size-fits-all approach and devise a political system that adjusts to suit the particular needs of each society.

Meanwhile, humanists refute the fallacy of a majority vote alone as being the mark of democracy. As I have said, the primary condition for humanist democracy is a humanist worldview. Without that, democracy is a sham. Many countries now allow citizens to vote in majority governments, but some of these are really hybrid democracies—that is, fronts for authoritarian regimes. As examples, I would point to the Congo, Iran, and even Russia. In the election of 2006, a majority of Palestinian voters elected leaders of Hamas, a terrorist organization, to form the new government. These countries or territories are not bound by humanist worldviews. In my opinion, therefore, all decisions that are made by a majority of voters in these hybrid democracies are suspect unless these decisions pass the test of the humanist code.

At present, the most important question is how to overcome the thick cover of antihumanist and antidemocratic values that grip so many countries. But I have confidence that we will overcome them and that a humanist democracy will become the universal ideal. Even now, people in many countries demonstrate in the streets for democratic reforms. Humanists can help them by explaining the entelechial process, proposing legal reforms to promote it, and pointing out the dismal historical record of totalitarian or other dictatorships. The Internet, moreover, will help us do these things—although our enemies use the same Internet for their own purposes.

Chapter 6

THE EVOLUTION OF DEMOCRACY

Modern democracy, the rule of humanist law, did not emerge suddenly. The earliest democracies, as I have said, were probably hunting-and-gathering societies of the Paleolithic. As a self-conscious experiment in large-scale societies, though, democracy has evolved over the past twenty-five centuries in the minds of philosophers.

Direct democracy, the first experiment in government by the people, began in Athens. Before long, though, it collapsed into tyranny. In my opinion, its failure can be explained very easily. Participants—a small segment of the population in any case—simply voted on every matter of public importance. The majority ruled. There were no checks and balances, to use modern parlance. The Greeks lacked any overarching ethical or philosophical principle, such as human rights. This is why the Greeks allowed no appeals for second thoughts.

After a few decades, therefore, Athenian democracy began to favor the few. Moreover, it began to favor the lowest common denominator among those few. Aristotle and Plato compared the system to mob rule (even though the "mob" in that case, unlike the "mobocracy" that frightened their early American imitators, consisted only of the richest and most powerful citizens). Among the most famous victims was Socrates.

Constitutional, or representative, democracy is a refinement of direct democracy. Its eighteenth-century advocates had clearly learned from the Greek pilot project. Founders of the American republic, for instance, soon realized that they needed a Bill of Rights, a series of amendments to the Constitution that was designed to prevent tyranny of the majority. By doing so, they established in all but name a humanist code.

Western philosophers of the eighteenth century were able to think of human rights for only one reason: the Enlightenment. Unlike the Renaissance, the Enlightenment was not simply a revival of interest in ancient philosophy. It was a new departure that emerged from a new situation: the prevalence of secular skepticism (even though some of these philosophers considered themselves either Deists or were members of secularizing religious communities). Far from relying on any insights from religious tradition, French philosophers either challenged or openly attacked religious tradition—including the Bible. It was this cultural environment of intellectual freedom that produced political freedom.

Among the overarching principles that the Enlightenment valued, two are of particular importance here. The first was human rights, an idea that emerged overtly in the eighteenth century but had intellectual roots that went back much earlier. Thomas Aquinas, who based his philosophy, known as natural law, on that of Aristotle, acknowledged the supremacy of revealed (divine) law in connection with the knowledge necessary for salvation, but promoted close observation of nature for all other kinds of knowledge. The intellectual heirs of Aquinas use natural law to this day in connection with ethics. In debates over the family and other institutions, for instance, they argue teleologically that nature's purpose—the natural purpose of marriage, say, or sex—defines what is right or wrong.

Enlightenment philosophers revived natural law, usually severing it from any connection with divine law, and enshrined it in pivotal documents such as the American Constitution. "We hold these truths to be self-evident, that all men are created equal ..." These truths were self-evident to philosophers of the Enlightenment, relying on observation of nature rather than on revelation, because they could see that what makes people unequal are not natural flaws in their essential humanity but the unnatural "chains" that society imposes on them. Therefore, people should all have equal rights under the law.

Not everyone grasped the radical implications of this philosophy. Educated landowners, especially in the South, came to believe that all white people (or at least all white landowners) should be equal under the law, but drew the line when it came to black people. Thomas Jefferson acknowledged that it was wrong to own other human beings but refrained from actually freeing his slaves. Some people denied that black people were fully human in the first place. It took a civil war to correct this flaw in the early republic—and another hundred years for most Americans to accept the full implications of equality under the law.

Today, natural law is unfashionable once more. Those who still advocate it often find themselves at odds with other philosophers, those who care more about personal "autonomy" than they do about the collective good (let alone nature, except in the sentimental sense of endangered species that need us to preserve them). Postmodernist philosophers argue that natural law is naive at best and sinister at worst, because no one can actually "read" nature without doing so through personal or political biases. What might seem objective, they conclude, is really nothing more than subjectivity masquerading as objectivity.

These philosophers do argue for human rights, especially in connection with the United Nations, but they have established no coherent or universal philosophical foundation for those rights. In effect, therefore, they simply *assert* that this or that group of people "have" (should have) this or that right.

Governments, especially Western ones, adjust their laws to suit the needs of gay people. This is a good thing in itself, because gay people have entelechial processes just as all other people do and therefore need the law to foster their self-actualization. But governments seldom worry about what adjusting those laws might mean for society as a whole. This is not necessarily a good thing, because personal self-actualization through individual or group rights can conflict with collective self-actualization through the collective rights of society as a whole.

The current stage of democracy's evolution requires a much more complete integration of humanism. In addition, it requires better ways of deciding conflicts between personal rights and collective ones. I refer not only to the ways in which legislators pass laws but also to the ways in which jurists interpret them. This is not a new problem. In the nineteenth-century Dred Scott case, for instance, the United States Supreme Court effectively denied the full humanity of slaves. But the problem will remain in one form or another as long as the courts must rely on the competing claims of expert witnesses.

Bias is still a major factor in the legislatures and the courts. Laws and decisions are not necessarily based exclusively on empirical evidence. The International Court of Justice had to decide on the legality of a wall, for instance, that the Israelis had built to counter terrorist acts against its civilian population. This court, backed by popular opinion in many countries, decided that the wall was illegal, because it was likely to hinder the creation of a Palestinian state. This suggested to me that public perceptions of justice were more important to the court than one obvious fact: Israel's need for security from attack by implacable enemies. In this case, neither side relied exclusively on empirical evidence. The Israelis could not prove that the wall would solve its problem, although that seemed likely. And the court could not prove that the wall would hinder the creation of a Palestinian state.

The next stage of democracy will be humanist democracy. It will be based exclusively on evidence from the study of human nature. All legal decisions will reflect likely results according to scientists. In that badly needed future system, anything considered just will conform to the humanist code. The humanist society will not permit legal sophistry, political biases, or even scientific theories to obscure justice.

The sense of justice will be beyond legal definition, in other words, as a function of the healthy entelechial process, and therefore beyond personal or group interests. Physicians do not believe in the efficacy of any drug based on theory alone. Why should legislators or jurists? And yet the latter often believe precisely that.

No constitutional declarations or protections can in the long term stand up against antihumanist attacks on democracy. Antihumanist sophistry, well-aimed propaganda, axiopathy, and legal loopholes eventually wear out humanist defenses as long as the latter remain at the abstract level, as they do under the representative constitutional system.

I believe that democracy should be explicitly grounded in the givens of nature. In that case, anyone could tell whether a law or its interpretation actually conforms to objective truth and therefore to the humanist code and the entelechial process. Only when laws do so will people know that democracy is secure. Humanism supports the current representational democracies by providing additional empirical support for them. Without that support, these systems would remain vulnerable to abuse, whether intended or not, due to sophisticated legislation or court rulings that would undermine it.

Humanist democracy, therefore, would *enhance* existing democracies, not replace them. Above all, the purpose of democracy is the self-actualization of the greatest number of its citizens, or the humanist society.

Democracy has made great strides over the millennia, the greatest so far being due to the Enlightenment in general and to natural law in particular. This has allowed the founders of American democracy, for example, to foster the expectation of "life, liberty, and the pursuit of happiness" (the Canadian equivalent being "peace, order, and good government").[64] This democratic ideal is based on insight into human nature and is thus a humanist ideal as well.

The more democratic or humanist any country becomes, the stronger and more prominent it becomes. But experience has now shown that when democratic and humanist principles are left to the mercy of powerful people, these principles tend to be colored by political fashion and therefore to negate their original and underlying functions. But we have reached a new stage in the evolution of democracy, because we can now test the justice of any legislation or legal decision by how well it actually serves the entelechial process.

Chapter 7

HUMANIST RELIGION AND LAW

Both religion and law must foster self-actualization. Ideally, Western religion does so by allowing people opportunities to experience holiness, or the sacred. Eastern religion does so by allowing people to experience enlightenment.[65] Law does so by allowing people freedom for the "pursuit of happiness."

The ideal, unfortunately, is not always the real. Antihumanist tendencies in religion and law sometimes get the upper hand. As a result, religion and law have often been used to diminish freedom and thus to support tyranny. This is what I have called *axiopathy*.

We can now avoid this problem with *onto-sociology*, a method that uses empirical evidence to distinguish true (humanist) interpretations of religion and law from false (antihumanist) ones. The method consists of two steps. First is to posit the humanist bias. Second is to establish what is best for society according to the humanist code. If the method is used correctly, we should be able to avoid the anomaly of religious or legal institutions being hijacked by demagogues—that is, people who try to justify their own arrogance by appealing to destructive interpretations of either religious or legal principles. Both steps rely on natural givens and are therefore beyond personal whims. Both prevent destructive interpretations, ones that lead to tyranny and exploitation, by insisting that the only legitimate interpretations are those that are best for society in the circumstances.

One corollary of this method is to prevent any powerful elite from having exclusive authority for interpretation. This is why courts, for example, routinely consult experts from a variety of fields—including scientists[66] (or possibly to laypeople who know enough about science).[67] This method would bring the best features of all religious and legal systems. At the very least, it would eliminate all the evils that have been done in the name of either religion or law. In short, it would bring about a humanist society.

The separation of religion and state was a good way to begin removing axiopathy. The trouble is that religion plays a primary role in sustaining democracy. The founders of American democracy understood the need for a religious civil society, one that would produce the moral fiber that every society needs. Their goal was to separate religion from government in particular, not to separate it from public life in general. Americans have made a wrong turn by trying to root out every last trace of traditional religion from public life while leaving secular religions—political ideologies—in place. I refer, of course, to humanist religion, which has been purged of any axiopathic elements. By providing people with this alternative, we would at least provide them with the kind of choice that any healthy democracy requires.

One example comes immediately to mind. Terrorism is generally defined as killing civilians for political causes. Humanists are interested in both the end and the means. As for the end, we believe that fighting against a democracy and for a dictatorship—either with or without resorting to terrorism—is inherently wrong. This is what made the 9/11 attack wrong from a humanist point of view. The same principle would apply in conflicts between two dictatorships; it would be wrong to fight for the more oppressive regime against the less oppressive one.

As for the means, a humanist must choose one that minimizes loss of life. But war is war, and we must accept the inevitability of some casualties. Those who attack civilians are always terrorists— unless, of course, they do not deliberately do so. Underground movements that attacked the Nazis during World War II were all justified, because they were trying to liberate people from tyranny.

Chapter 8

HUMANIST ECONOMICS

Modern economics, Leslie Lipson has noted, is not really an integrated science but a conflict between various interests. "This has led to one sector winning this battle and another coming from behind to win the next, without any of them necessarily improving the human condition in general."[68]

Humanist economics, on the other hand, changes all this by closing the circle. It brings a new and absolute goal to the purpose of economics. The self-actualization of as many people as possible, within the context of the humanist code, is not subject to conflict. It permits new theories and experiments, and frees economics from the dead ends of unverifiable hypotheses and seductive ideologies. The merit of any theory or policy depends not on its apparent theoretical soundness alone, but on how well it works to bring about a humanist society. If it works, then we accept it—but only as long as it continues to work.

"If it works" is thus the sine qua non of humanist economics and would allow for a mix-and-match strategy, choosing this or that theory for its usefulness in any particular situation. This flexibility distinguishes humanist economics from both capitalist and socialist ones, which usually serve the interests of dominant classes. Humanist economics could end false expectations—notably the ones that have led to dictatorships—by forcing all new theories, like all new drugs, to undergo a period of testing. Moreover, it could invite innovators to solve economic anomalies. With humanist economics, for instance, it would be possible to nationalize assets, a socialist way of starting up new industries if the private sector were unable to do so. Additionally, humanist economics would indicate when we no longer needed that policy.

To give a more extreme illustration, we could try communism for a while in very primitive economies; this would help those societies catch up. Early communism eventually improved the growing but still backward Russian economy, though at a heavy cost in lost lives and political repression. In some societies, we could redistribute land and turn peasants into successful farmers while compensating landowners with bonds of long-term maturity and preventing excesses against those landowners.

But communism, like any other system, would eventually become dysfunctional, as it did in both the Soviet Union and China. The economic system that I am describing would guide a country in that situation safely toward a humanist society while maintaining all democratic rights.

Humanist economics is a way of managing the material wealth of a country to achieve the self-actualization of as many people as possible. This is the gold standard by which to measure all economic activities. But the underlying goal is to create a humanist society. This invariant goal is the only one that legitimates the ownership of property, limits of wealth, economic power, and so on.

The whole system is like a farm. Farmers use seed, fertilizer, water, labor, and other inputs to achieve the greatest yield for their land; everything that they do must be measured and justified by that goal. Humanists devote all of their efforts to the self-actualization of as many people as possible. The same applies to their efforts in connection with education, public health, and all policies that involve economics. It is a classic two-dimensional gestalt of ends and means with a credibility and accuracy that fully equals those of the natural sciences.

Here are the priorities of a humanist economist. One is to redistribute wealth. For the entelechial process, everyone needs at least some material means in order to survive and maintain dignity—that is, be able to function constructively as part of a humanist society. By the same token, society as a whole must protect itself from any situation in which a few people have most of the wealth or power. This would diminish the entelechial process, endanger all the rights that go with it and eventually destroy society as a whole. So the primary criterion must be a ceiling as well as a floor for how much wealth anyone may have.

In the early twentieth century, for instance, Karl Polanyi warned that economic policies that are detached from society—from the social good—would end up destroying society. There must be something above economics, he said, something that directs it toward the service of society. To ignore that goal would be to invite not only despair but also resistance and even political upheaval. He believed that fascism was the result of social despair, which was in turn was the result of a "disembedded" economics.[69] In short, market or self-regulating economics is a self-destructive fantasy.

Humanists support his point of view. In fact, they add that *anything* affecting the human condition must affect society; all social forces must answer to and be justified by the good of society.

One argument against the redistribution of wealth is that it rewards "idleness" while punishing innovation and therefore productivity as well. But humanist economists do not derive the right to wealth from innovation or productivity in isolation. They do so as from the overarching structure of society, which allows each section of the population to contribute its best. We must place society's integrity before that of any individual. Society has a right to regulate the distribution of wealth in a way that benefits everyone—or at least most people—and thus that preserves democracy and opposes plutocracy.

Another priority is to ensure public health. Most modern countries have elaborate health-care programs, although not all make sure that adequate health care is actually available to everyone. As a humanist, I believe that health care is a basic right of every citizen. How could anyone have a vital entelechial process without it? But the extent of health care depends on society's wealth and priorities, and these can fluctuate.

Education, another requirement of the entelechial process, presents the same problem. The right to education, like the right to health care, would be a basic right of everyone in a humanist society. Modern societies invest heavily in education to produce intelligent and productive citizens. Humanist economists must allocate the amount of money that society spends on education. As always, due to society's many priorities, it is a question of deriving the highest benefit from the lowest investment.

How useful, then, is capitalism? And when does it stop being useful? Capitalism, like democracy, is a sine qua non of humanism. Within the safeguards provided by the humanist code, capitalism ensures the freedom of everyone. Otherwise, though, it can take more out of the economy than it should. Characteristic signs that capitalism is in trouble would include the following: growing gulfs between the rich and the poor, increasingly powerful governments; increasingly powerful interests controlling the mass media; failing educational systems; regressive taxation; restricted competition due to giant trusts; destruction of the natural environment by unregulated industries; and organized crime. The presence of some or all of these problems would mean the dawn of a pathological phase—what I call *patho-capitalism*. But humanist economists can distinguish easily between healthy and unhealthy capitalism. The former is democratic and necessary; the latter is predatory and intolerable.

Humanist economists would likewise be able to tell us how far we could go in exploiting the natural environment without lasting damage. By now, we are all familiar with the many ecological problems of our time: air pollution, water pollution, global warming, desertification, the extinction of many species, and so on. We need an international body to help us monitor industrial growth. And this suggests to me the need for a humanist world government, which would control industry and protect the planet.

The laws of nature are relentless. Just because we sometimes violate those laws and continue to survive does not mean that we can continue doing so forever. Humanist economics is the only approach to economics that receives its basic goals from human nature and fully accommodates itself to nature.

Chapter 9

HUMANIST EDUCATION

The purpose of humanist education is to convey the exact relation between the entelechial process and human rights. This is the universal message to all peoples in all cultures.

Humanist education, like every other venue of humanism, is rooted in the need to understand all aspects of human nature. Humanist educators, therefore, must tell students how the motivational system works and how to achieve self-actualization by applying that knowledge. Most important for my purpose here, educators must tell students how institutions can help them achieve self-actualization and the consequences of failing to do so.

As a humanist, I believe that everyone should accept the entelechial process as a factor of life that is beyond dispute. That in turn would lead students to the conclusion that democracy is a natural outgrowth of the process, not merely one political ideology among many. There would not be much room for choice on this matter. Students would have to choose between democracy and autocracy, for instance, in one form or another.

The entelechial process is a natural given and therefore the only thing that gives meaning and legitimacy to behavior. It is the ultimate criterion to be used in solving all moral, legal, political, or social problems that impinge on universal human rights. Humanist education would be the source, therefore, from which all virtues flow. Democracy is not a genetic gift; it is a special technology or process that people must learn.

When it comes to politics, humanist teachers would help students to differentiate between democracy and autocracy. Students would learn from history why democracy is the only legitimate form of government. They would learn to move beyond traditional left-wing and right-wing politics to see the continuum between them and humanism. Everything that moves politically toward humanism and is therefore likely to create and sustain a humanist society is, of course, good from my point of view. Political systems on both the left and the right are usually based on utopianism, which means that they ignore inconvenient aspects of human nature. Humanism is different, because it relies more fully on empirical evidence.

Human rights are derived from human nature, students would learn, and therefore from the entelechial process. Those rights resemble the effects of food, exercise, and fresh air on physical health. They also affect spiritual health, not only physical health. And that is the goal that humanists would set before students as future citizens: to give as many people as possible material and physical security, freedom from ignorance and fear, freedom of religion and expression, and so on.

A yearning for democracy is growing stronger in many parts of the world. Think of Latin America, parts of Asia and Africa, and especially the formerly communist countries of Europe. Yet most attempts at democracy have been only partially successful at best due to education systems that do not promote humanism.

Good ideas have a way of spreading. This was true even in ancient times, when communication was not as quick and easy as it is now. Students no longer rely exclusively on teachers and textbooks for ideas. They turn to the Internet. Even though the Internet makes all ideas—both humanist and antihumanist—easily available, I believe that young people will eventually favor the former over the latter. If humanist educators ignore the Internet, however, then their adversaries will win the day. Humanists should use the Internet, like the classroom, to explain the relation of humanism to nature in general and how the entelechial process works in particular.

Because humanism is based on human nature, it offers many liberating solutions to some of the most vexing philosophical questions that students encounter in social studies. One of these is the important question of the purpose of life. By presenting the entelechial process, humanist educators would invite their students to test the hypothesis in everyday life.

Students in various courses would find that the idea of self-actualization is hardly new. They would recognize it in the works of Aristotle, the Upanishads, the Talmud, and so forth. (For more about that, see appendix A.) But they would learn that the humanist version is new in some ways. For one thing, it is an overarching theory that relies on a single instinct governing and coordinating all motivations: a unified theory of motivation. (For more about my own expansion of that theory, see appendix A.)

Humanist teachers would prepare students to be citizens of the world, because doing so would show students that social relations are as synergistic within one community as they are with the whole world. Humanists believe that education unites the whole world into one community, regardless of divergent views. To put this another way, a humanist education would promote the moral and democratic goal of solidarity across all borders. That is because humanists believe that people cannot achieve their full potential if others—within their own society or in the world as a whole—cannot do so.

Humanist educators could participate also in courses on philosophy. Think about the controversy between determinism and free will. Some philosophers and theologians have emphasized one, some the other. A humanist would confirm both. Students of philosophy, I suggest, would find this debate very interesting and useful. The entelechial process consists of fourteen constants, which are instinctive and therefore determined by nature. But behavior in response to those motivations is a matter of free will. Free will, in fact, means nothing more than choosing the best way to achieve self-actualization.

Another controversy of interest to students in philosophy courses is the historical one concerning Cartesian dualism. Descartes argued that mind and body are separate things. Others have argued that they are two aspects of the same thing. For humanists, the problem is easily solved. The entelechial process cannot exist without a body. Nor can it exist without a mind. Therefore, it can exist only within us as psychophysiological beings. Like most modern philosophers, therefore, humanists reject Cartesian dualism (though not necessarily all forms of dualism).

Now, think about the more recent philosophical controversies over feeling and thinking. Should students trust one or the other?

As a humanist, I would say that they should trust either or both to the extent that either fosters the entelechial process in any particular situation.

What about students who are good at both mathematics and music? Which career should they choose? One solution would be to think about market conditions and the prospects of finding jobs. Another would be to go with the emotionally satisfying career. Humanists would try to find a balance.

And what about the roles of emotion and reason during elections? Usually, candidates who make emotional appeals do better than those who rely on intellectual ones. But voters should have learned in school that they need reason to confirm that an emotional appeal is justified. Clearly both should enter into any decision. Humanists would teach students that feeling and thinking are synergistic, not irreconcilable.

Chapter 10

HUMANIST JOURNALISM

As a humanist, I believe that the function of journalism is to support a democratic society and promote the creation of a humanist society. Citizens need journalists to provide them with accurate reports that are based on fact, not on personal whim or bias. Moreover, citizens need journalists to monitor government activities and other institutions. Finally they need at least a few journalists who can suggest new solutions to social or other problems.

Plato said that tainted knowledge can be as dangerous to spiritual health as tainted meat or drink is to physical health. Few have challenged that apt assertion, but few have been able to agree on what constitutes "tainted knowledge." They have failed to agree because of their failure to understand human nature. Humanists therefore feel obliged to revisit this problem. At no time in history, perhaps, have we needed a solution more urgently than we do now.

Most people—except, unfortunately, for postmodernists and political ideologues—agree that objectivity and truth are vital features of good journalism, so humanist journalists need only define these words precisely. As I have already explained, humanists derive the definition of any value by discovering its function in the entelechial process within the context of the humanist code.

How would objectivity and truth serve the interest of a humanist society? In the case of objectivity, it does so most effectively when humanist journalists arrange the facts accordingly. Is this not propaganda? It is propaganda to the extent that it relies on a point of view. That is, it selects and arranges objective truths in ways that promote humanism.

To report the news objectively during World War II would have been to report news that supported the Allied countries and not the Axis countries. Why? Because the Allied countries were defending democracy, which humanism supports; the Axis countries were defending totalitarianism, which humanism opposes. The two should not be on the same level.

Most people on the Allied side would have agreed. They would have done so because they had taken a moral position against totalitarianism and not because they claimed to be objective and morally neutral. They would have claimed instead that an objective evaluation of war aims on each side would have supported their moral claim.

Humanists would have argued, on the other hand, that their own claims about war aims on each side were rooted in nature, not moral bias, and therefore that those claims *coincided* with claims that were rooted in objectivity.

This is how humanists explain what appears to be a contradiction. Bias and objectivity are opposites, to be sure, which means that people cannot embrace both at the same time and still make sense. But nature and objectivity are not opposites. Bias against the entelechial process and objectivity can never coincide, but nature and objectivity can.

Similarly, humanists say that human life is objectively inviolable. To ensure the entelechial process, society must apply some basic humanist rules. Apart from anything else, society must acknowledge that extreme poverty and tyranny are unacceptable.

The second vital feature of humanist journalism is truth. But what is truth? For humanists, truth is a view of facts in connection with the entelechial process and the humanist code. But truth is sometimes more than a collection of data. It has a strong moral dimension that bears on human destiny. For instance, I must not reveal the hiding place of an intended victim; lying to a murderer serves a greater good than telling the objectively verifiable truth.

To be credible, journalists must rely on facts. As everyone knows, people can manipulate facts easily for personal or political purposes. But manipulation—bias—is not always a bad thing. For humanists, it can be a good thing if it promotes a humanist society. Only antihumanist or antidemocratic bias is a bad thing.

Consider the following analogy. If a new drug might help patients, then physicians prescribe it—unless, say, the latest clinical trials reveal that its success is more apparent than real, or that it cures one thing but creates new problems as well due to deleterious side effects. At that point physicians stop prescribing it. If a bias toward physical health is part of science, why should a bias toward spiritual health not be part of sociology?

The humanist bias is to look at human problems from the viewpoint of human nature. This is the primary task of humanist journalism. Without a natural and fixed standard, of course, all viewpoints would be equally valid. There would be no absolute good and evil; these would be no more than a question of convenience or power. For humanists, that natural and fixed standard is the entelechial process. Arguing for the good would lack credibility without that sustaining fact—which is what humanist journalists would openly promote, especially in their coverage of conflict between democratic societies and nondemocratic ones.

Although the world religions have provided us with clear notions of good and evil, some religious people have always managed to distort those notions in ways that serve their own purposes. So have secular people, for that matter, in the name of political ideologies. Humanists call these people *axiopaths*. Among the tasks of humanist journalists, therefore, is to make readers aware of the axiopaths at home and abroad.

Humanist journalism imposes a special responsibility to look at the world and report on it in connection with humanist ideals, and thus make it possible for readers or viewers to distinguish between good and evil, democracy and totalitarianism, and so on. This is what many people—those postmodernists who reject objectivity—now promote as "advocacy journalism" (though not necessarily in favor of humanist ideals). As I have already said, it is a moral outlook and therefore biased, not objective. According to humanists, though, nature supports this particular bias. This approach allows humanists not only to report the news but also to advocate responses to the news.

To express all this succinctly, I have provided the following two-dimensional gestalt equation: humanist journalism = humanist bias (purpose):selection and presentation of facts (variable means). This expresses the idea that humanist journalism is two-dimensional. It has an invariable end and a variable means.

Humanist journalists would affirm the first dimension by asking what the best solution to any problem is—in other words, what would result in the self-actualization of as many people as possible and thus bring about a humanist society? The second dimension involves means. The means are variable in order to promote flexibility, innovation, and creativity—always subject to testing against empirical evidence.

Consider how journalists covered the war in Iraq. Some journalists supported the war, arguing that it would end the suffering of minorities, curb terrorism, and promote democracy in the region. This was an implicitly humanist position. Other journalists opposed the war, arguing that it originated in American duplicity or greed and that it would further destabilize the region.

After an early victory over Saddam Hussein, American troops settled in for a long war against insurgents. As the casualty figures mounted, it became clear that this was a guerilla war for which American leaders and American troops were ill-prepared. Public criticism of the war, its origin, and its conduct soon erupted in the press and on television.

After a while, many American journalists condemned the war. In effect, they helped the insurgents by fostering the assumption that Americans had lost heart in the war effort and were incapable of winning. In other words, the journalists' implicitly antihumanist bias worked against their nation's vital interest in spreading democracy.

Some readers might argue that a humanist bias in journalism could be impractical or unpopular. But so what? Journalists do not implement policy. They merely convey information that could help those who do implement policy. Those who implement policies, in turn, cannot for long ignore objective and true reporting and sound ideas as revealed by humanist journalists.

The correct humanist response to reverses caused by the insurgency in Iraq would have been to admit that Americans must adapt to guerilla warfare by establishing better ways of collecting intelligence, making it legal to bomb all targets where terrorists hide—including among civilians—and meting out the maximum punishment for terrorists on trial. Humanist journalists would have had to convince the public that not doing these things immediately would exact a much greater price later on.

I turn now to extreme forms of antihumanist journalism. Some represent no more than the private views of a single psychopath, as in the case of Adolf Hitler or of a superterrorist such as Osama Bin Laden.

The problem with antihumanist bias in journalism is that it implicitly denies the supremacy of the entelechial process and any respect for human rights as decreed by nature and affirmed by the humanist code and other human-rights documents. These journalists have contempt for democracy, respecting only the interests of absolute rulers. Their basic ideas are hostile, therefore, to the true public interest.

To describe this phenomenon, I use the word *pravdaism*, which originated during the Stalinist era among Russian dissidents and conquered people in eastern Europe. The Russian word *pravda* means truth—that is, truth from the perspective of dictators who know that they can enforce it by brutal force. But I extend the use of this word to include extreme antihumanist journalism everywhere. I include terrorists such as al-Qaeda and hate groups that operate on the Internet.

I make an important distinction between propaganda in general and pravdaism in particular. The aim of propaganda is to disseminate ideas of any kind: true or false,[70] overt (as Nazi or Communist ideology was) or covert (as capitalist ideology is),[71] totalitarian or democratic, secular or religious. The aim of pravdaism is more specifically to disseminate lies that undermine the creation of a humanist society and therefore humanist journalism as well.

Here is an equation that should make my point clear. Pravdaism = promotion of sociopathological causes (bias):coercion by denial of truth (means). The purpose of pravdaism is to promote a sociopathological cause by denying truth. Pravdaism is false because of its goal, therefore, and not because of the facts that it presents. So there is a difference between the journalistic bias of humanism and that of pravdaism. The former promotes collective self-actualization for as many people as possible; the latter promotes personal power for a dictator.

I suspect that the only reason for resorting to pravdaism is to acquire or maintain power—which includes wealth and safety from enemies. This is why most dictators employ pravdaism, at any rate, no matter what their ideologies purport to do. The humanist response to pravdaism is to protect the dissemination of truth in the same way that public-health departments protect the food supply: by avoiding contamination.

One factor that might well lead to pravdaism in our society is part of the fallout from postmodernism and the political correctness that it supports. I refer to relativism, the refusal to be "judgmental" or "discriminatory" by distinguishing clearly between good and evil. At the moment, many journalists accept this premise consciously. They call it, as I have already noted, advocacy journalism. As the counterpart of "engaged scholarship," it openly encourages subjectivity as the goal—that is, ideological bias instead of objectivity. The result really is something like pravdaism but probably much more sophisticated than anything that the Soviet Union ever produced. Other journalists, perhaps most of them, remain dangerously unaware of what is at stake.

Those who practice pravdaism might champion a popular cause, but only, ironically, as a cover for antidemocratic measures. They often marshal facts combined with strategic falsehoods, rely on stereotypes, and capitalize on public ignorance, religious allegiances, and whatever else suits their purposes.

Humanist journalism and pravdaism represent the two poles of journalistic bias: the healthy and the sick. Most present-day journalists combine the two. There is no pure humanist journalism, nor is there a pure pravdaism. In the most humanist of publications, we can find some antihumanist biases; in the most pravdaist of publications, similarly, we can find some popular humanist ones. The most important question for humanist journalists is how to distinguish clearly and readily between the two.

Humanist journalism leads to healthy spirituality as nourishing food leads to physical health. Pravdaism leads in the opposite direction. It might even champion death over life if that becomes expedient.[72]

Pravdaist journalists pose an internal threat to democracies at least equal to the external one of military might. They do so by trying to control the minds and hearts of their intended victims through systematic deception. They invariably compliment the military or economic powers of aggressors. Even if only for that reason, humanists should urge people to recognize these journalists as specialized enemies within.

In order to protect the public and the integrity of humanist journalism, we could try a humanist rating system similar to bond-rating or movie-rating systems. In this way, journalists could use the Internet to guide the public in choosing newspapers, news magazines, and news shows. Competition among the producers of health products has resulted in many new and medically useful products—although it has also resulted in many fraudulent claims, which is why we need governments and courts to oversee all claims. Humanist journalists would apply objective standards to monitor the mass media. This system would give democracy a head start in making its case by giving maximum credibility to those who plead for humanist solutions to world problems and orient people toward the goal of building or maintaining humanist societies. And it would counteract the chaos of clashing worldviews at the United Nations, which is nothing more than a league of sovereign states, each pursuing its own divergent interests.

To summarize, relative to the unified theory of motivation, journalistic biases are of three kinds: humanist, activist and pravdaist.

The humanist bias hews strictly to the facts as they relate to the humanist code—that is, to human nature. This is why it always opposes the violation of humanist principles.

The activist bias serves the interests of particular political parties, ideologies, or causes. It could include partially humanist and antihumanist biases at the same time, depending on how zealous it happens to be. Most journalists in democratic countries are now in this category.

The pravdaist bias is strictly authoritarian and therefore supports despotic or terrorist causes. It is openly hostile to democracy and humanism. It has no regard for humanist or activist versions of the facts. Rather, it manufactures facts to suit its own purposes. It facilitates the most extreme types of tyranny.

Chapter 11

AXIOPATHY AND SUFFERING

As a humanist, I define the word *suffering* as anything that has a negative effect on the entelechial process and thus becomes a dysfunction. Unlike suffering in general, which can be caused either by natural forces or moral agents, *evil* is always caused by moral agents and always involves injustice. It is always a specific moral category, therefore, even though people can experience its effects in physical or other ways.

Hurricane Katrina was a natural disaster, for instance, but not a moral one. It involved suffering but not evil. Government response or lack of response to Katrina, on the other hand, was the result of human choices. To the extent that those choices were the result of indifference to suffering, though probably not outright malice, they could be considered evil.

Both evil and suffering belong within constant D of the unified theory of motivation: reactions and depletions. Without this humanist theory, it would be impossible to pinpoint the exact effect of any negative act on any specific part of the entelechial process (although any act or lack of one always affects it as a whole). Alcoholism could affect physical health (constant C4) by attacking the liver or other organs. It could affect performance on the job (constant B2) and family and social relations (constants B3 and B4) as well as other constants, depending on the severity of the case.

Thus, we can see the entire entelechial process by locating the specific constant that is affected most and treating that area, using the norms attending one or more of those constants. This would make the diagnosis and treatment of psychological dysfunctions much easier than it is now, concentrating treatment on a specific area of consciousness rather than diffusing it over the entire psychological spectrum.

The entire category of dysfunctions contained in constant D divides into two minors: Constants D1 and D2. The first is an essential negative reaction to the extent that it deters negative behaviors from going to constant D2, which is the constant of self-destruction. Thus fear (constant D1) of fire or lung cancer would discourage smoking in bed. Constant D1 includes essential reactions that prevent far worse consequences.

This leaves what I have defined as constant D2, depletions and pathogenesis, which includes all reactions that are alien to the entelechial process. It is the repository of all suffering and evil, no matter what the cause. The cause makes no difference, because it always represents a diminution of the entelechial process. Evil and suffering either deter (D1) or diminish and destroy (D2) the process—including the creation of a humanist society. In an ironic way, evil reinforces the process. I am thinking of an old saying to the effect that the gods make mad those whom they wish to destroy—making them violate human nature, in other words, to the point of either destroying themselves or allowing others to destroy them. When tyrants murder people en masse, in short, they provoke resistance.

This brings me to a very important but very ancient question. Why do bad things happen to good people or good societies?[73] The most common answer in Western religion has been that the cause of suffering, whether due to evil or nature, is a mystery.[74] But that is for another book. In this one, I want to discuss only forms of suffering that we can understand and eliminate.

According to my classification system, there are three broad causes of suffering: natural problems (constant D2.1); psychological problems (constant D2.2); and social problems (constant D2.3). I rank these according to the damage that they cause. The most dangerous are totalitarianism and ecological degradation.

Under natural problems, I include all the obvious ones: storms, earthquakes, plagues, and so on. Although we cannot eliminate those problems, we can mitigate the damage that they cause. Unfortunately, people are now exacerbating or causing natural afflictions by degrading the natural environment. By definition, this is not entirely a natural affliction. It is more of a social problem, in fact, which is why I will discuss it elsewhere.

I turn now to psychological problems. In *The Unconscious God*, Victor E. Frankl discussed the possibility of self-transcendence through the "will to meaning."[75] When the latter is frustrated, the result is lack of self-actualization, unrealized potential, or what he called "noogenic neurosis." It is the most widespread spiritual malaise or psychological deficiency, and the underlying cause of problems such as psychosomatic illness, social upheavals, and totalitarian tyranny.

Though a natural given, the entelechial process is by no means automatic. Almost any problem can stall it. Fundamental to ensuring self-actualization for most people, therefore, is a clear understanding of this process and how to manage it. This is where the unified theory of motivation comes in.[76] Noogenesis is not widely understood or even widely recognized as an immediate threat.

On a much larger scale than natural and psychological problems, social problems can involve evil. We can control or eradicate most, fortunately, by applying the unified theory of motivation. Society is where good and evil clash. Axiopathy is what happens when evil wins. This is what concerns me most in this book.

All social systems fit onto a continuum between two ideal types: the humanist and the antihumanist, or the democratic and the autocratic. The sole function of the former is to ensure the self-actualization of as many people as possible. The sole function of the latter is to ensure the perverted self-actualization of a dictator. I have already said a great deal about democracy, so I turn my attention now to autocracy.

In autocratic states, power resides in a ruler and a small ruling class. Actually, *nondemocratic* would be a better word, because by no means all of these societies have been ruled by autocrats—that is, dictators who acknowledge no law apart from their own whims. In chapter 2, I explained that the prototypes of modern dictators were not their immediate predecessors but chiefs and kings of the very early Neolithic period. Some states in recorded history have been worse than others, of course. But my primary interest here is in the modern dictators of totalitarian societies, because they (along with pandemics) probably represent the greatest threat to human survival.

Even though anti-Americans like to say that the United States is the greatest threat to world peace, the evidence points clearly to dictatorships such as those of Iran and North Korea. I say this partly because democracies seldom resort to war against each other. They do so primarily to defend themselves against dictatorships.[77]

Chapter 12

ANATOMY OF DESPOTISM

The aim of this chapter is to explain autocracy as a universal menace, the antihumanist principles that it relies on, and the brutality and deceptions that it uses to achieve its ends. I will discuss only modern dictators, because they present an unprecedented threat due to the rise of terrorists and weapons of mass destruction. These weapons—including suicide bombers—proliferate and become more deadly by the minute with the financial and political help of dictators. This situation forces democracies to defend themselves. That situation, in turn, threatens not only democratic liberties but also human survival. Therefore, humanists must eliminate despotism, gradually, through peaceful means. (I will discuss all this more fully in the third volume of this trilogy.)

All authoritarian systems have three basic goals. They enforce all three at any cost. They manipulate the public with illusions and, when all else fails, with lies. Humanists would express the system as a two-dimensional gestalt project of ends and means as follows: despotism = the desire for maximum power, maximum material wealth, and elimination of enemies:coercion by physical force and coercion by lies. This equation means that despotism is an absolute political system. The most important effect of the system, from a humanist point of view, is to deny the entelechial process and therefore human nature—which is why it never lasts very long unless people are aware of no alternatives.[78]

I see three kinds of authoritarianism: relatively benign ones, severe ones, and totalitarian ones. All absolute rulers, as I say, want power and at least some measure of additional wealth, territory, or fame.[79] In addition, they want to eliminate those who stand in their way as enemies, either real or imagined. Humanists believe that these are the basic motivations of observers, that they differ from each other only in the extent to which they are willing to go in trying to attain these goals and in their secondary motivations.

Benign autocrats try to serve the needs of their people without risking much of their own power. They are limited by their own abilities and by the attitudes of their people. They are usually peaceful too, partly because conflict would undermine the stability on which they rely.

Benign dictators are not necessarily evil. They must sometimes take action not only to protect their own power but also to protect their people from chaos or conquest. But power can easily corrupt anyone, including even the best-intentioned autocrat. The system itself often requires some evil means to attain good ends.[80] In some cases, repressing dissent is justifiable, but not often.

Here are a few of the many leaders who fall into this category: Solomon of ancient Israel; Hatshepsut of Egypt; Marcus Aurelius of Rome (or even Augustus for that matter); the Buddhist Ashoka of India; the Muslim Akbar and Dara Shukoh of India; Elizabeth I of England; Joseph II and Franz Ferdinand of Austria; Alexander II of Russia; and Gustav III of Sweden.

Severe autocrats rely more heavily on ideologies, whether religious or secular. They are less likely to hesitate before repressing dissent or conquering or demanding sacrifices from their followers. Sometimes even they find it hard to distinguish between their presumably lofty ideological aims and their selfish personal ones. These are very dangerous rulers, not only to their own people but also to other peoples. If unchecked, they can become autocrats of the third category. Here are a few examples: Mahmoud Ahmadinejad of Iran (even though he was, technically, elected), Kim Jong-Il of North Korea, and Saddam Hussein of Iraq.

Totalitarian autocrats are absolute rulers, unlimited by any religious or ideological checks, although many of them make grandiose religious or ideological claims. They prefer to gain a minimal level of popular support; even though they can repress dissent, they would prefer not having to invest their resources in doing so. As a result, they rely heavily on propaganda to pacify people.

Because their ultimate and conscious aim really is to acquire personal wealth, power, and fame, totalitarian autocrats are eager to conquer and exploit other nations. They have no respect for human rights, of course, either at home or abroad.

I call these leaders axiopaths. As a humanist, I urge people to discredit them and countries to wage war against them. Appeasing them is a great mistake, because doing so has the effect of making them all the more aggressive. Better to prevent them from gaining power in the first place.

Here are some of the most obvious examples of totalitarian autocrats: Adolf Hitler of Nazi Germany, Joseph Stalin of Soviet Russia, Benito Mussolini of Fascist Italy, and Mao Zedong of Communist China. Clearly these leaders, who saw human life as a renewable resource to use as they saw fit, were the most extreme and therefore the most dangerous ones.

These categories are flexible. Some leaders move from one to another. Throughout history, some rulers have either taken or inherited absolute power and used it justly. What are now called world religions originated as attempts to limit the power and behavior of absolute rulers. They imposed ethical restraints. Rulers who went beyond those restraints were—and were considered even at the time—legitimate targets for assassins and revolutionaries. Rulers could no longer do whatever they pleased without facing the consequences. They ruled in the name of God or the gods, true, but only as long as they maintained a system based on divine teachings.

You can see this attitude emerging in prophetic works of the Bible and continuing throughout European history, but especially in England after the nobles forced King John to sign the Magna Carta and thus to begin the long process that led to parliamentary rule. Something similar occurred with the Confucian writings of China, the Upanishads of India, and many other sources.

Nonetheless, recorded history indicates that even these restraints were inadequate by modern standards. Not all rulers were personally concerned about the welfare of their people. Those who were may have been good rulers for their times or places, but they were not humanists. And no matter how wise or compassionate, they could not ensure the orderly transfer of power to others of their kind. A humanist democracy, by contrast, would rely on a democratic system instead of luck.

People must learn and keep learning about democracy. It does not succeed automatically. Nor is it exclusively about voting, as most people think, although that is an essential ingredient. For humanists, democracy is mainly about knowledge of the entelechial process and thus of human rights. Without this knowledge, democracy would not work, much less endure. Eventually, it would break down and leave a political vacuum for despotism, if only to maintain order. Consider the attempted introduction of democracy in Iraq after Saddam Hussein was deposed. Most people, at least those in the Shi'ite majority, were willing and eager to vote but had no training in how democracy works—that is, in the need for a strong civil society.

I believe that a humanist democracy would be a great challenge but also the most effective antidote to any form of authoritarianism. Humanism must come first chronologically, then voting. From the humanist perspective, authoritarianism is a crime against humanity to the extent that it suppresses or denies legitimate human rights. Anyone who has experienced tyranny knows how to recognize it without humanist proselytizing. Humanist democracy requires only the essential knowledge of how to bring it about.

The first step, therefore, is to promote humanist education and—in our time—the Internet. Perhaps the most effective way to explain and spread humanist democracy in the long term, though, might be through new interpretations of religion. Most religions at the moment allow one form of axiopathy or another. They usually serve the cause of ruling classes, clergy, or absolute rulers.

We live in a religiously polarized world: secularism versus fundamentalism. This is true not only at the macrolevel of West versus East, moreover, but also at the microlevel of conflict within Western countries, where religious decline correlates with liberalism, not conservatism. I am not surprised by the growing success of fundamentalist religions, because these fill the vacuum left by secularism. Religion supplies the ideas for a very powerful instinct (the axioma complex, constant A1). (See appendix B for more details on the power of religion.)

The ideal time to reinterpret religion in humanist terms is therefore now, when secular ideas are strong and religious ones weak, because those who already gravitate toward secularism would gravitate toward a humanist reinterpretation of religion. This would go a long way toward producing a new generation to support democracy through religion.

Conclusion

HUMANISM AND SCIENCE

I will conclude this book with a concise summary of my theory about the relations between humanism on the one hand and science on the other. I define science very broadly here as the search for systematic and verifiable knowledge. Knowledge of the entelechial process, which I presented in the first volume of this trilogy, makes verification possible.

Kurt Goldstein's theory of personal self-actualization and the works of those who followed him, including my own unified theory of motivation, make possible for the first time the development of self-actualization on an empirical basis. The same goes for collective self-actualization in connection with humanist democracy. Social scientists can now have a common goal: realizing the entelechial process. With this in mind, they can study values as functions of a humanist society and subject to empirical evidence—sometimes even to exact measurement. They can confirm or refute any proposition concerning the individual or society according to how it actually affects that process. The implicitly humanist side of religion, for instance, becomes clearly distinguishable from the axiopathic side. The humanist code supplies common values, derived from nature, to unite all people regardless of cultural diversity.[81] Most important, from my perspective, is that humanism supplies the worldview for world federation.

I have tried to show that humanist religion satisfies the need for either union with God or experience of the mysterious universe as well as the need for a worldview that fosters self-actualization for the greatest number of people. It is now possible to test any religious teaching scientifically according to how it actually affects individuals and societies.

Consider the Ten Commandments. These introduced a moral law into Western history. Despite frequent setbacks, they (or the worldview that produced them) spawned religions that have, in turn, changed the direction of history. Humanists see the highlights of history as the moral advances of humanity as a whole and the worst setbacks as the moral catastrophes of authoritarian systems. History is the story of all humanity. All individuals and all nations are related to each other, so the moral history of each is that of all.

The secular humanist code, derived from human nature, contains everything that we need to create or sustain democracy. It is now possible to test all social systems—political, economic, religious, and so on—according to how they affect the entelechial process. The function of economics, for instance, is the production and distribution of wealth in ways that lead to self-actualization for the greatest number of people. This does away with conflicting economic theories. The reference point of economics is how to produce wealth and how to distribute it effectively.

To find the humanist definition of any value, in fact, we need only ask ourselves how it fosters or hinders the entelechial process. In this way, even ethics is now something like a science: systematic and readily verifiable.

Similarly, humanism suggests a new approach to history. We need only ask how historical events have affected the entelechial process. History is the struggle of all humans to survive and flourish against extraneous forces both natural and human, so everything that happens or does not happen must be related in some way to the entelechial process.

I cannot say strongly enough that modern humanism works side by side with science. Advocates of humanism, like those of natural law, believe that human rights rely not on mere belief systems but on natural givens. These, they believe, makes possible the unity of all of humanity without the loss of valuable rights. After that, it is a question of trial and error on how best to implement the best policies.

It was the world federalist movement that attracted me back in my youth. But it did not have a common value system, which made me certain that it could not succeed. As I saw the situation, it is impossible to unite the democratic with the autocratic in one federated union. No organization or society could be united without a common worldview; otherwise, we would have nothing more than a multicultural Tower of Babel—which is what I saw.

In the next and final volume of this trilogy, I will present a universal system of human rights, how it can effect a genuine unity among democratic societies, and how it could ultimately create a humanist world federation.

Appendix A

THE UNIFIED THEORY OF MOTIVATION AND THE CONSTANTS OF HUMAN BEHAVIOR

My goal here is to help readers who are unfamiliar with the first volume in this trilogy.[82] This appendix is a summary of that first volume, which showed that we can transform the social sciences, beginning with psychology, into natural sciences.

Social scientists have always wanted to make their disciplines as rigorous as those of natural scientists. Their problem has been that people are much harder to study than gravitational fields, geological deposits, chemical compounds, and so on. For one thing, there are moral and legal limits on how far researchers can go in experimenting with people. This means that social scientists cannot use the standard scientific mechanism: replicating results in a laboratory and thus either verifying or falsifying their hypotheses (although scientists in some fields do not use that mechanism). Moreover, people are so complex and present so many variables that even statistical analyses are imprecise—or, at the very least, lead to imprecise conclusions about human behavior.

My unified theory of motivation is an attempt to level the playing field, as it were, by identifying the many aspects of human behavior that are universal and therefore not variable (along with those that are). I call these nonvariable aspects of human nature *constants* and add that each includes several *minor constants*. The result is a description of human nature in the biological sense of *nature*.

My hope is to make a true science of psychology (and, by implication, other social sciences such as sociology, economics, and political science) and to lay the foundation for a humanist society—which, by definition, is based on human nature in that same sense.

A humanist society would be one in which as many people as possible can attain self-actualization. To put it another way, a humanist society would be the collective version of personal self-actualization.

In this new science of humanism, the entelechial process is the foundation of society. The family is the smallest and most basic unit of society. The individual's entelechial process, however, is an irreducible and self-contained biological given that, with the entelechial processes of other individuals in structured and institutionalized relationships, such as the family or the clan, forms society.

Because people cannot change their basic biological, social, and psychological needs and motivations, these being not only universal but also invariable, society must adapt to them. Before continuing, I will try to explain that. People can and do adapt to society in some ways. Moreover, there are limits to the extent that society can or should adapt to individuals. It is a two-way street, not a one-way street.

Taking one point of view are sociologists who promote the theory of social constructionism, which came into fashion during the 1980s. (It is now under attack by sociobiologists, who go even further by arguing that human existence hinges not on the family or the individual, but on the *gene*.) Social constructionists assert (because they cannot prove) that society is infinitely adaptable, that it can be anything we want it to be.

Underlying that supposedly academic assertion, though, is a political goal: to legitimate the social revolution that they happen to want. They want women to work outside the home, for instance. Therefore, they argue that children do not need mothers who stay at home; all children need is "quality time" with their mothers. They want women to be "autonomous." Therefore, they argue that divorce is a good thing not only for women but also for children. They want women to have sole custody of children. Therefore, they argue that children do not need fathers at all. They want gay people to marry. Therefore, they argue that two parents of the same sex are just as good for children as one parent of each sex, and also that biological ties are of no importance. In fact, the erosion of biological ties and a consequent increase in social fragmentation underlies all of these things.

But my point here is that these sociologists and like-minded psychologists argue that everything, even fatherhood and motherhood, amounts to nothing more than a *social construct* (what others would call a social experiment) and can therefore be bent this way and that or even discarded without any ill effects. The big winners have been adults, mainly women. The big losers, of course, have been children, and therefore society.

But now, after all those years, the longitudinal studies have been completed. The statistics are in. And the news is bad for both children and society. Almost every major social problem involving children—crime, drug addiction, unwanted pregnancy, low academic achievement, learning disabilities, and so on—is directly attributable to the social experiments that have been going on in the name of social constructionism.

Society is *not* infinitely malleable. There are limits. These limits, like those of the individual, are due to human nature, not individual human nature in this case but collective human nature. Natural laws govern human societies. Given those natural laws, every society must have laws or customs that encourage the young to marry and have children. Every society must have laws or customs, in other words, to protect the family. Any society that chooses not to heed nature will pay the price.

Some things work with groups and other things do not work. Every society is an experiment in some sense, but some experiments work better than others. Historians and anthropologists have shown which ones have better track records. We could try to reorganize ourselves as a matrilineal society, for instance, and we might even succeed. But we would probably pay a high price for doing so, because historians and anthropologists have shown that matrilineal societies tend to be very unstable; they present inherent problems. So, caveat emptor.

Encouraging everyone to strive for self-actualization must therefore be the basic function of society. From this, it follows that governments must serve the needs of citizens. Democracies do so. Dictatorships do not and cannot therefore command the loyalty of citizens. They endure for a while, but only by imposing themselves by brute force. They are doomed in the long run because they must work against human nature.

The unified theory of motivation consists of fixed motivations and "movable" behavior. The basic motivations are natural givens and universal. Each plays a definite and necessary role in the achievement of self-actualization. Behavior, on the other hand, is variable, subject to personal choices as a result of free will. The best behavior in any circumstance is the one that leads to the highest degree of self-actualization within the context of the humanist code. A bad choice would be one that defeats the code.

The task of *onto-psychology,* or the psychology of being (that is, of being healthy), is to collect the best data possible for each constant, as derived from healthy achievers.[83] Societies differ in their demands for behavior to satisfy the various constants. Societies are not all equally good at helping people achieve self-actualization. A society that respects a woman's right to develop her talents and allows her to work outside the home is better, from my perspective, than one that does not. It all depends on how this or that form of behavior plays out in connection with the entelechial process. This is the criterion that allows humanists to differentiate between right and wrong forms of behavior.

But let me get down to business. I have identified four major constants and fourteen minor ones. All of these, working together, generate self-actualization.

Major constant A motivates people to seek self-actualization through knowledge of the entelechial process. It includes four minor constants.

Minor constant A1 motivates people to internalize a collective worldview. I call it the *axioma complex* to suggest that it has the authority of a religio-political system. Its values unite the community, determine its identity, and make possible its existence as a recognizable unit. The healthiest society would be a humanist society, because humanism originates in human nature as the drive toward self-actualization on a collective level. This was improperly understood until the advent of Kurt Goldstein, and later on of Abraham Maslow, Viktor Frankl, Erich Fromm, and many others.

Minor constant A2 motivates each person to create a personal value system. Working with the collective worldview creates the conscience. Everyone has free will and can therefore choose personal values that work either with or against the collective worldview. The healthiest personal value system would be informed by humanism, once again, because it would originate in human nature as the drive toward self-actualization on a personal level. Every violation of the conscience, however, registers as a strong negative response under D1 (which I will discuss in a moment). This is the home of empirical science too, as distinct from the tautological science of religion contained in the axioma complex, or constant A1 above.

Minor constant A3 motivates each person to seek self-knowledge or identity. Even though identity includes all aspects of behavior, it focuses primarily on labor for men and reproductive labor for women. Women derive their identity as women directly from nature. Men do not; they derive it from culture—that is, their jobs or careers. But there is a significant overlap. Fatherhood is a major source of identity for most men, and motherhood is not the only source of identity for most women. Choosing well, clearly, leads to self-actualization.

Minor constant A4 motivates people to seek knowledge of the larger world and therefore of how to survive and even thrive within it. To achieve self-actualization, people must know, apart from anything else, how the entelechial process works. This is the constant of all education, which people require for specialized jobs as well as to acquire knowledge they need for self-actualization.

Major constant B motivates people to adopt the behaviors that are necessary to achieve self-actualization. It includes several minor constants.

Minor constant B1 motivates people to learn. For my purpose here, I would stress that they must learn in particular about human nature and the human rights that flow from them. Otherwise, they will be unable to attain either personal self-actualization or collective self-actualization (in the form of democracy).

Minor constant B2 motivates people to seek satisfying labor. This is the primary channel of self-actualization for men but a necessary secondary one for women as well. Under ideal conditions, work would not be a hardship; on the contrary, it would be a challenge and a pleasure. In that case, it would lead to spiritual growth and therefore to maturity.

Minor constant B3 motivates people to seek satisfying family lives. This is the primary channel of self-actualization for women but a necessary secondary one for men as well. This motivational difference between men and women, complementarity, makes family life and even social cohesion possible. Family life is based on interdependence, not personal autonomy; each member of the family contributes to the self-actualization of all others.

Minor constant B4 motivates people to establish social commitments. The entelechial process reveals that democracy is the best political system. In addition, it reveals which people are likely to become the most valuable friends and associates. Being linked to other people is a precondition for self-actualization.

Major constant C motivates people to ensure their own survival by maintaining physical health. It includes several minor constants.

Minor constant C1 motivates people to eat and drink. Like all living things, people must do these things. In fact, they must satisfy hunger and thirst before any other needs. The ultimate goal is not mere physical survival, of course, but self-actualization.

Minor constant C2 motivates sexual activity. Like most animals, people have sexual urges. Sex is basically a physiological urge that we require for reproduction. But it has additional functions and therefore demands satisfaction even after we have reproduced ourselves.

Minor constant C3 motivates self-defense. People need to protect themselves from assaults of various kinds, including those of oppressive regimes. The form of government that offers most security is democracy, especially in countries that value the rule of law more than personal autonomy.[84]

Minor constant C4 motivates people to maintain good health, both physical and psychological. One way is to create or maintain a democratic political system. Most democracies are very effective in providing social services: free medical care, low-cost housing for the poor, labor codes to ensure fair hiring practices, safety standards for workers, employment insurance, statutory holidays, vacation, maternity or paternity leaves, and so on.[85]

Many nondemocratic countries provide the same services to their citizens, sometimes even more generously, but at the heavy cost of denying them freedom.[86]

Major constant D motivates people to do evil things. Sometimes its power is due to frustration in connection with one or more of the other minor constants, including moral failure. It includes two minor constants.

Minor constant D1 includes all motivations that deter people from abandoning the quest for self-actualization: hunger, thirst, sexual frustration, fear, pain, and so forth. These are "good," because they tend to protect the essential and more positive things that I have already mentioned. Moreover, this constant motivates the conscience to react against thoughts such as revenge or aggression.[87]

Minor constant D2 motivates people to malicious (what Maslow calls "evil") behavior. Although the previous constants provoke specialized behaviors that lead toward self-actualization, this one provokes behavior that leads away from it, and therefore against the self, society, or both.

Any frustration, physical or psychological, can trigger malicious behavior. As a result, every society finds ways to prevent it. Healthy societies are generally successful, because they satisfy the needs of most people most of the time. But even healthy societies must resort also to deterrence and punishment.

And if people cannot direct their malice against society, they can often direct it against themselves, sometimes, possibly, in the form of psychosomatic disease.

This constant is essential in the overall drive toward self-actualization, ironically, because it motivates people to avoid anything that might lead them away from self-actualization. That reasoning does not apply to dictators, of course, who are in the grip of this constant and therefore not interested in creating a society that fosters self-actualization for anyone but themselves.

The "constants" listed here are both universal and verifiable. One constant is the social instinct (B4), which determines, among other related matters, the formation of a government that can lead to the self-actualization of most people. This is in accordance with the humanist code, which not only determines the moral and legal systems of society but also influences the consciences of every individual within it.

The entelechial process is the locus of all research on human nature, both individual (psychology) and collective (sociology, economics, political science). People have free will but can use it only to choose between promoting the entelechial process and violating it—to put it another way, the choice between good and evil. Without a firm understanding of good and evil, which this unified theory of motivation makes possible, free will would be like a ship without a compass.

The social sciences, like most of the natural sciences, began as descriptive projects. Over the past two centuries, though, the natural sciences have become controlling projects. The same thing is now possible for the social sciences. This will prove to be a turning point in the social sciences, I believe, making them into credible sciences.

Because the entelechial process it the only nonvariable aspect of behavior, according to this unified theory, we now have a constant against which to measure every other aspect of behavior. We can define all values—both virtues and vices—in relation to their functions in the entelechial process. We can identify something virtuous, for instance, by selecting and arranging specific facts in connection with their benefits to the entelechial process. This approach clearly shows that democracy, for instance, is more virtuous than autocracy; the former enhances the entelechial process and the latter does not. Eventually, this approach would lead to the creation of a humanist and democratic world federation, its legal system based entirely on human nature and therefore valid for all humans.

All behaviors affect the entelechial process in a way that can be studied objectively. A man might think that it is fun to get drunk, for example, but then find that getting drunk has serious consequences—ones that affect his entelechial process. The latter progresses or regresses no matter what he thinks, affecting everything that he does or does not do.

Appendix B

THE POWER OF THE AXIOMA COMPLEX: GOOD V. BAD RELIGIONS OR WORLDVIEWS

The axioma complex (constant A1) is the most influential and powerful instinct within the entelechial process. It consists of political and religious systems that impose laws. It governs the collective psyche and therefore informs its character.

The most important feature of any political or religious system is that people accept it subconsciously as based on axioms, first principles from which all others are derived. When communities accept those principles in the form of commandments, say, these communities strengthen the bonds that hold people together as communities—which is what makes these worldviews strong, whether for good or ill.

The mind works this way because people need to find meaning in connection with the purpose of life, the desire for justice and peace, or the mystery of innocent suffering and death. With that in mind, every society establishes a moral or legal code. To do so, it must rely on some proposition that requires no elaborate justification and proof. People must accept that proposition on faith, in other words, as something that has supreme and possibly superhuman authority. Without establishing such a proposition, society would have to function without any recognized authority. Order would collapse, leaving society like a ship without its rudder.

The axioma complex, therefore, is the source of law, ethics, custom, religion, and spirituality. Every society must acknowledge it and even defend it if necessary.

But a scientific worldview demands evidence for every axiom. For humanists, this means evidence that it fosters the entelechial process—which is to say, that it fosters humanism and democracy while undermining antihumanism and dictatorship. Humanists believe, moreover, that scientific study will always undermine axiopathic religions—those that promote the worship of a god who supports or even demands tyranny. In fact, they believe scientific study will always support humanistic religion. Humanist religion, in short, is necessary for any humanist society. The unified theory of motivation separates wheat from chaff: humanist spirituality from axiopathic spirituality, political or religious freedom from political or religious tyranny.

The struggle against axiopathic religion in particular has a long history. In modern times, critics have demanded evidence for first principles. If they fail to find these, they say so. For Marx, all religion was axiopathic, the "opium of the people," an "illusion," and "wishful thinking." Attacks on humanist forms of religion, on the other hand, are like attacks on eating or any other instinctive behavior.

People must have a worldview, whether political or religious; as soon as one disappears, another appears. The new worldview might be more humanistic than the earlier one, or it might be less humanistic. How to tell the difference was a matter of trial and error before anyone knew about the unified theory of motivation.

Attacks on religion fail, for instance, if they rely merely on lack of evidence for a first principle. That is because most people do not really care about a first principle's origin; they care only about its implications for them in daily life. Science works in the same way. It relies on axioms, or first principles, but most scientists are interested mainly in applying those to practical problems in their own research. That is where the evidence counts.

The legitimacy of any worldview depends, therefore, entirely on its implications in daily life and not on the superficial appearance of an abstraction.[88] When political leaders or religious prophets promote tyranny, humanists immediately recognize them as demagogues or false prophets.

Once we know what or which political or religious principles work well—those that foster the entelechial process—we can use that knowledge effectively to promote a humanist society. And once we know which political or religious principles do not work well—those that foster an axiopathic society—we can use that knowledge effectively to provoke change.

Many people have attacked religion as a whole by dwelling on axiopathic religions alone, as if there were no others. These attacks are laudable, because they are attacks on abuse in the name of some political or religious worldview. Even so, they fail to solve the underlying problem of human need—that is, the need for a worldview to unite society. By denying human nature, we end up creating a tyrannical regime, even if its original axiom is intrinsically true. The entelechial process lies not in the intrinsic worth of the worldview's original axiom but in the final authority on what is necessary for human flourishing.

What about the assumed conflict between science and religion? The former studies human nature, but the latter prescribes a way of life that promotes the essence of that nature. The same thing is true of science and political movements, including those that are officially hostile to religion. Scientists can predict axiopathy, in other words, and thus save us from axiopathic political or religious worldviews.

But the axioma complex is not so powerful when it comes to the individual. It represents the collective worldview, not the personal one. That is where the conscience, constant A2, comes in. It represents the worldview of someone with free will. People who have the same axioma complex might or might not have the same personal values. Everyone in a democratic society is free, of course, to escape the bond of the society's collective worldview. But the axioma complex's power remains decisive for society and can therefore override personal dissent.

Any durable civilization must be grounded in humanism at the level of the axioma complex. Here is one example. Jews have not only survived as a nation, even in exile, but have disseminated humanism to Christian, Muslim, and secular humanists. Even today, Jews are usually successful in the struggle for self-actualization, especially in democratic countries.

The most outstanding recent example of a country that fosters humanist power is the United States. It has two advantages: the

Protestant religion and a constitutional system. Countries to the south have many natural resources but not those two things. Latin America is undergoing a religious and political revolution, however, and this gives us reason to hope for the spread there of humanism and democracy. Many other countries have access to humanism through either religious or secular sources. The latter would include the humanist code, of course, but also the United Nations Declaration of Human Rights.

Humanism is the sine qua non, I believe, of democracy. Consider the situation in Iraq. From a humanist perspective, American military intervention there was justifiable. It toppled Saddam Hussein. The attempt to create a democracy there without first creating a humanist foundation for it, though, was a predictable failure. American officials should have given power, immediately but temporarily, to a benign dictator and backed the latter directly or indirectly with military force. The Iraqis had never known democracy or established the civil society on which any democracy depends. Humanism comes first, in short, not democracy.

Humanism is by no means alien to Islam. From its inception, Islam practiced human values that made it the most civilized and powerful force in the world. Gradually, however, absolute rulers with authoritarian values began to appear, thus gradually lowering and weakening Muslim societies. Today Islam is in the grip of strong authoritarian values, which prevents it from establishing a democratic system that can only be based on humanist values as contained in the humanist code.

Islam, like any other great religion, potentially contains enough humanist values to lift the people toward a democratic system if correctly interpreted. Such interpretations can be given to Muslims through the Internet, as one example. There are many Muslims who are humanists in their values and could communicate this healthier interpretation of religion to other Muslims, and thus give them the most basic tools for democracy, without which authoritarianism will continue to hold sway.

Early Muslims drew on humanist sources that originated not only in the civilization of the Bible but also in those of Greece, Rome, Persia, India, and China. Muslims often cooperated with Jewish and Christian minorities (though less often with Hindu minorities).[89] Gradually, though, Muslims turned inward and against the humanism that earlier generations had preserved and continued.

The axioma complex is a primary tool and a primary problem in the spread of democracy. Democracy has been very successful in postwar Japan (which had no democratic tradition but did have a highly educated population), postwar Germany (which had a democratic experience of only twenty very troubled years but also had a highly educated population), and postcolonial India (which had learned and even inherited much from the British). So far, though, democracy has been less effective in Russia (which experimented with it very briefly after the Soviet collapse).

The axioma complex can work both positively and negatively. Britain is a stable democracy. In 2007, though, a few Muslim citizens, some highly educated, planned suicidal terrorist attacks in Glasgow and London. The same mayhem has occurred in France, Germany, and many other Western countries, in addition, of course, to Saudi Arabia, Egypt, and many other Islamic countries.

Thus, good and evil derived from the axioma complex, including all religio-political ideas, depend entirely on interpretation, and that means self-actualization within the context of the humanist code for the greatest number of people.

NOTES

[1]   The Library of Congress has many works in Hebrew by Ben Ish Hai (listed as Joseph Hayyim ben Elijah al-Hakam, ca. 1834–1909). The following books are English adaptations: Daniel Levy, Days of Peace: *The Ben Ish Hai on the Coming of the Messiah, the Return to Zion, and the World to Come* (Jersualem: Yeshivat Ahavat Shalom, 1999); Daniel Levy, *Israel and the Nations: The Ben Ish Hai on the Uniqueness of Israel and Its Path through History to the Final Redemption* (Nanuet, NY: Feldheim, 1998); Daniel Levy, *Between Heaven and Earth: The Ben Ish Hai on Faith, the Nature of Evil and the Final Reckoning* (Nanuet, NY: Feldheim, 1995); Daniel Levy, *The Challenge of Wealth and Poverty: The Ben Ish Hai on Wealth, Poverty, Charity and the Torah's View of Money* (Nanuet, NY: Feldheim, 1996); Daniel Levy, *Dawn of a Nation: The Ben Ish Hai on the Early History of the Jewish People from the Bondage in Egypt to until They Enter the Holy Land* (Nanuet, NY: Feldheim, 1997); Daniel Levy, *If I Forget Thee: The Ben Ish Hai on the Land of Israel, Jersualem and the Holy Temple* (Nanuet, NY: Feldheim, 1998); Daniel Levy, *In the Service of the King: The Ben Ish Hai on Repentance, Closeness to God, Holiness and the Redemption of Sparks* (Jerusalem: Yeshivat Ahavat Shalom, 1996); Nehama Consuelo Nahmoud, *Parables from Bagdad* (Brooklyn: Lightbooks, 1981); *The Light of the Ben-Ish Chai on Megillat Esther*, tr. Yerachmiel Bratt, (Philadelphia: Xlibris, 2003); Yaacov Kahn, *Golden*

Apples: Parables of the Ben Ish Hai, trans. Shaindl Weinbach (Brooklyn: Mesorah, 1991); Shmuel Hiley, *The Halachoth of Ben Ish Hai* (Spring Valley, NY: Feldheim, 1989).

[2] Kurt Goldstein, *Human Nature in the Light of Psychopathology* (New York: Schocken, 1963).

[3] Alexis Carrel, *Man the Unknown* (New York: Harper, 1935). "The sciences of inert matter have made immense progress, while those of living beings remain in a rudimentary state" (27). "Since the natural conditions of existence have been destroyed by modern civilization," he says elsewhere in the same book, "the science of man has become the most necessary of all sciences" (29).

[4] Kurt Goldstein, *The Organism: A Holistic Approach to Biology Derived from Pathological Data in Man* (Boston: Beacon Press, 1963).

[5] Abraham Maslow, *Motivation and Personality* (New York: Harper and Row, 1954).

[6] Joseph Sassoon, *Self-Actualization* (Montreal: Humanica Press, 1988).

[7] Despite the obvious parallel, I am not drawing on utilitarianism. Like Jeremy Bentham (and John Stuart Mill), I call for "the greatest happiness for the greatest number." But my theory has a different origin.

[8] "They [self-actualizers] have for human beings in general a deep feeling of identification, sympathy, and affection in spite of occasional

anger, impatience or disgust ... Because of this they have a genuine desire to help the human race. It is as if they were all members of a single family." Maslow, *Motivation*, 217.

9 Abraham Maslow, *Motivation and Personality* (New York: Harper and Row, 1954).

10 Actually, organized religion originated for several reasons. Among them was the need to propagate the spiritual insights of individuals from one generation of society to another, and thus not have to keep reinventing the wheel. Knowledge of this kind and many other kinds could be stored and made accessible to every generation in the forms of ritual and myth.

11 Charles Templeton, *Farewell to God: My Reasons for Rejecting the Christian Faith* (Toronto: McLelland and Stewart, 1996).

12 See Joseph Sassoon, *Self-Actualization* (Montreal: Humanica Press, 1988), 257.

13 There is a difference between the axioma complex (Constant A1) and the axiomatic force. The former refers to religious, philosophical, political, or other texts that affect behavior. The latter refers to the influence of religious, philosophical, political, or other leaders on their followers. This happens in all spheres of life: following the will or example of a business leader, say, or imitating a sports hero. It is the force of an admired or feared model. President Eisenhower used it when he promoted civil rights and even sent in federal troops to enforce them. In a less dramatic way, government officials promote blood drives.

Clearly, malevolent leaders can use the axiomatic force just as effectively as benevolent ones.

[14] Some immigrants bring antihumanist perspectives from homelands at war with modernity. These perspectives overcome the humanist features of their religions. Consider the case of Zacarias Moussaoui. Convicted of terrorism, who denied being part of the 9/11 attack but expressed solidarity with those who were. And he denied being mentally unbalanced. But many Muslim immigrants integrate successfully, at least by the second or third generation. Even the most mature democracy would fail to delegitimate the most extreme forms of antihumanism. So the integration of immigrants depends on the degree of antihumanism that they have brought with them as well as the opportunities they have to absorb humanism.

[15] Democracy ideally coincides with humanism, which is a broader category, but not necessarily. All democratic societies are humanist ones, but not all humanists societies, or at least protohumanist have been democratic ones.

[16] What about the need to explain death and other natural phenomena? That is probably a later development, both historically and existentially. Some early religions, such as that of Homeric Greece, produced myths that can be interpreted as primitive science—or, more likely, primitive psychology. But these myths are probably very recent in the larger historical context. References to fertility and weather in Greek religion, for instance, indicate the agricultural (and, to some extent, pastoral) needs of Neolithic communities. Other religions of the same general period, such as that of ancient Egypt, produced myths and rituals

that can be interpreted as primitive responses to the fear of death and therefore primitive attempts at science. But these too rely heavily on the agricultural imagery associated with the death and resurrection of plants—that is, crops. The earliest strata of biblical religion reveal only a vague interest in what happens to people after they die. Like the Greeks, the early Israelites believed that a soul of some kind survived death but lived in a shadowy realm called *she'ol*. It took many centuries for the Israelites to consider other possibilities. It was only in the rabbinic (post-biblical) period that Jews came to believe in two contradictory notions about life after death: resurrection of the body on a day of judgment (at the end of history) versus immortality of the soul (which exists in eternity, both before and after history).

[17] So far, the record for political ideologies serving as secular religions—national socialism, for instance, and communism—is not exactly encouraging.

[18] Hinduism emerged gradually from a past so remote that its origin cannot be traced to a single founder. Judaism emerged gradually, too, but much more recently. Instead of one founder, it has several: Abraham, Moses, Isaiah, Yohanan ben Zakai, and so on.

[19] This does not mean that those others lack ethics and therefore encourage unethical behavior. It might mean only that what we call "ethics," a branch of theology or philosophy, is subsumed under some other category. In the case of Judaism, for instance, that would be sacred law (*halakhah*). Many small-scale societies do not link personal behavior with the requirements of divine beings. Personal behavior is just as carefully regulated as it is in large-scale societies but by other

means, usually kinship systems. To have inappropriate sexual relations, for instance, would not be "sinful" but shameful, an offense against not the gods but the elders or the ancestors. People would not turn to the gods for moral instruction, therefore, but for other things such as abundant crops or protection from poisonous snakes.

[20] From other points of view, of course, it is not entirely legitimate. The first anthropologists were either imperial functionaries and traders or Christian missionaries. In other words, they were *outsiders*. Even though they were interested enough to describe foreign cultures, they usually did so on a very condescending basis. They looked down on the insiders, who seemed primitive and therefore inferior to Westerners. Their descriptions were tainted by Western smugness and arrogance, in other words, and therefore *subjective*. Later anthropologists realized that they could never fully understand foreign cultures without taking seriously the perspective of *insiders*—that is, of their informants. Living among them for lengthy periods, learning their languages, participating in their rituals, and so on, anthropologists began to see themselves not merely as observers but as *participant-observers*. And they adopted a method, called *epoché*, which was based on the school of philosophy called phenomenology. Relying on Edmund Husserl, this method required them to bracket out, as ruthlessly as possible, their own preconceived ideas and preferences. Only in that way could anthropologists even hear what their informants were saying and therefore be *objective* in response. (See C. Moustakas, *Phenomenological Research Methods*, Thousand Oaks, Calif.: Safe, 1994.) This method turned anthropology into a truly *empirical* discipline. No one can ever attain perfection in objectivity (or in anything else), but objectivity remains the goal of all trained anthropologists.

[21] Eastern religions are very different in this way (and in many other ways). Neither Hinduism nor Buddhism, for instance, relies on a hierarchy of authority or institutionalized power; both are therefore very "disorganized" religions. Even though Hindus believe that their ultimate goal is enlightenment (nirvana) and therefore liberation (*moksha*) from the cycle of birth, death, and rebirth, and thus from all social and political structures, they do not necessarily attain that goal within a single lifetime. Moreover, they try to seek that goal only in later life, after they have fulfilled their duties to society as parents, householders, and members of communities. These communities, the castes, are indeed arranged in a hierarchy of status. Buddhists are more radical in this respect. They live in communities because all people must live in communities. But only one community has any specifically Buddhist legitimacy: the monastic one (*sangha*). And even that community is intended only to train Buddhists seeking enlightenment and liberation.

In short, neither Hindus nor Buddhists invest leaders with the kind of authority that Western religions invest in bishops, priests, and ayatollahs, or even imams and rabbis, who are authorized directly or indirectly by their communities to interpret sacred law.

[22] Protestantism is linked not only with the rise of democracy but also with the rise of capitalism. This is probably the legacy of one particular form of Protestantism: the Calvinist tradition, which holds not only that individuals are masters of their own destinies but also that prosperity is a sign of election (predetermined salvation). The link is more remote, though, because not many capitalists, even early ones, have taken responsibility for making choices that affect society.

[23] Protestantism is linked not only with the rise of democracy and the rise of capitalism, moreover, but also with the rise of *secularism*. The early Protestants would have found that possibility beyond imagining, but they had already taken the first step toward secularism by rejecting the Catholic doctrine of transubstantiation. According to that doctrine, Christ's body and blood are present in the bread and wine served at every Eucharist (Communion service); Christ is physically present and sacrifices himself, in other words, at every Eucharist. According to Protestant doctrines, the bread and wine are merely symbols of an event that happened long ago and far away; Christ is not present and therefore does not sacrifice himself. By implication, the sacred is no longer present within a profane world. But if the sacred is absent, then so is the profane (which can be defined theologically only in connection with the sacred). That makes the world secular.

[24] I use the past tense for a reason. In the eighteenth century, individualism did not mean what it has come to mean in the twenty-first century. It involved the personal "pursuit of happiness," true, but not to the extent of abandoning responsibility for the community. At that time, individualism was always seen within the context of citizenship—that is, civic duty. In our time, it usually refers to nothing more than license for self-indulgence.

[25] The caste system is much more fluid than it ever was. The central government regulates it by assigning "reservations" to the lower castes; this amounts to affirmative action. Moreover, lower castes have lobbied successfully to have their status upgraded within the caste system; this amounts to upward mobility.

[26] Not many Jews condoned or supported totalitarian movements in the twentieth century. But there were some, at least in Italy. "Neither racism nor anti-Semitism had been part of Italian Fascism's formative principles and ideology. There were prominent Jewish fascists and anti-fascists, and membership in either had less to do with Judaism than other attributes such as class, region, generation, and ideological orientation." Franklin Hugh Adler, review of *Racial Theories in Fascist Italy*, by Aaron Gillette. *Holocaust and Genocide Studies* 18, no. 1 (Spring 2005): 127.

[27] No early state could have been totalitarian, actually, because none had a communication system that was capable of mass indoctrination or sophisticated bureaucracies and surveillance technologies that were capable of isolating and keeping track of every citizen. Beginning in the late fifteenth century, though, Spain became the prototype for all modern totalitarian states. To unify itself as a new nation-state, Spain used the Inquisition to eliminate political dissent, impose religious conformity, and even create racial purity.

[28] Humanism, as a moral code, applies to everyone. To the extent that Judaism is humanistic, therefore, it applies to everyone. To the extent that it is not humanistic—in its dietary laws, circumcision, liturgical order, and so on—it does not apply to anyone except Jews. The same is true of every religion. I believe that the ancient Israelites attacked only those aspects of other religions that they found morally (humanistically) offensive.

[29] Leviticus 19:18. (All biblical quotations are from the King James Version Bible.)

[30] Ruth 1:16.

[31] Ezra 10:10–11.

[32] For an excellent discussion of this problem by someone who prefers the universalist approach, see Kenneth Reinhard, "The Ethics of the Neighbor: Universalism, Particularism, Exceptionalism," *Journal of the Society for Textual Reasoning* 4, no. 1 (November 2005). Reinhard begins with a discussion of the debate between Hillel and Shammai and the former's "golden rule" (recorded in the Babylonian Talmud, Shabbat 31a), which is not quite as simple from this perspective as it might seem. To give you some idea of how important this conflict is in Jewish theology, philosophy, and ethics, check this search string on the Internet: *universalism, particularism, Judaism*. As of this writing, Google responds with no fewer than 23,500 Web sites.

[33] Isaiah 42:6, 49:6.

[34] 1 Samuel 15:3.

[35] 1 Samuel 15:23–33.

[36] The biblical authors were not anthropologists and did not necessarily understand foreign religions. Their many polemic tirades against idolatry, for instance, were based partly on a mistake: that idol-worshippers were stupid enough to believe that stone objects, which had been carved by ordinary people, were actually gods. But idol-worshippers knew perfectly well that these statues had been manufactured and were not gods. What they believed was that gods could be present either in

or near these statues, at least temporarily, for the specific purpose of communicating with worshippers, just as the Israelite God could be present in or near a bush, a mountain, and so forth. A few neighboring communities might well have sacrificed infants to gods such as Ba'al, but most neighboring communities probably did nothing that most people today would consider evil, let alone horrific.

[37] Isaiah 60:4.

[38] No religion can ever be thoroughly democratic, although some religions find it more useful for practical purposes than others do. That is because religion, like science or scholarship of any other kind, is ultimately about truth, and truth can never be established merely by counting heads. The majority of scientists or other scholars might agree about some theory, but agreement does not make them correct; the dissenting minority might turn out in the end to have been correct all along. The majority of Buddhists might agree about some doctrine, similarly, but that it itself does not make it true (consistent with the tradition, beneficial, and so on); the minority might turn out in the end to have been correct all along. In either case, moreover, no one at all might have guessed the truth.

On the other hand, many religious denominations find democratic mechanisms very helpful in an institutional or administrative sense. They hold elections for ecclesiastical offices and elect lay representatives to ecclesiastical boards, councils, and committees. Those elected to participate in making decisions, however, realize that these decisions are always provisional (at least in theory) and not absolute. Democracy is the best *political* system that we have, in short, but not everything is political.

[39] Vatican II documents make it very clear that "dialogue" is not a euphemism for "proselytizing." In them, the Roman Catholic Church acknowledges the legitimacy of other religions—the continuing legitimacy of Judaism in particular—and even expects to learn from them.

[40] The papacy's monarchical model of ecclesiastical government is undemocratic and therefore unacceptable to humanists. It has one advantage, however, over other models. Once a pope decides to change all Catholic textbooks or all Catholic prayer books to reflect a humanist approach to theology or to oppose an antihumanist one (such as anti-Semitism), he can do so immediately and thoroughly.

[41] In my opinion, France would benefit from the active presence of a humanist form of religion such as Protestantism, one that would focus on personal self-actualization and therefore complement secular humanism. Why would the French adopt a new religion? They might in order to establish a new spiritual and moral foundation. At the moment, France has entirely rejected the Catholic religion without adopting another one.

[42] The Buddha began with a rigorous analysis of suffering. The Four Noble Truths are based entirely on observation and reason. Although the Buddha acknowledged the existence of gods, he denied that they could be of much use to anyone. Like people but on a slightly higher plane, he said, the gods are seeking enlightenment. They might be able to help people with mundane problems such as famine or disease, but they cannot help people attain the ultimate goal of liberation from suffering, which is caused by craving for permanence (caused in turn by the illusions presented by our senses) in a world that is always in

flux. Theravada Buddhism, which prevails in southeastern Asia, has remained close to the Buddha's original analysis. Mahayana Buddhism and Vajrayana Buddhism, in eastern Asia and Tibet respectively, have been more innovative; some forms reduce the role of reason to a minimum. But they foster another humanist value: compassion. The ultimate goal is not to reach enlightenment, but to do so and then turn back into the world as a bodhisattva, which always involves suffering, and teach others the path to enlightenment.

[43] Confucianism, like rabbinic Judaism, values learning, tradition, order, and social harmony. Both are what one anthropologist called "Apollonian" cultures. Ruth Benedict, *Patterns of Culture* (Boston: Houghton Mifflin, 1934). But after reading the work of another anthropologist, I can see an even more important correlation between these two cultures: the urge to recreate on a microcosmic scale through ritual (*halakhah* in the case of Judaism and *li* in the case of Confucianism) the perfection of a cosmic prototype. Herbert Fingarette, *Confucius: The Secular as Sacred* (New York: Harper and Row, 1972).

[44] At first, the British believed in democracy at home but colonial administration in other parts of the empire. By the early twentieth century, however, most British administrators understood that they needed to prepare Indians for "home rule"—that is, training the Indian people to administer their own democratic government, and thus follow the path of other dominions such as Canada and Australia.

[45] This applies to all religious fundamentalism, of course, not only Islamic fundamentalism. But Islamic fundamentalism is more dangerous than other forms of religious fundamentalism, because the historical

and political contexts of Islamic countries have allowed fundamentalists access to much more power than in other countries. Otherwise, Islamic reformers—they were becoming increasingly active during the late nineteenth and early twentieth centuries—would have succeeded in establishing a liberal and democratic form of Islam.

[46] This expression, "people of the book," has nothing to do with any love of learning or books (although it sometimes has that connotation among Jews today in reference to themselves). It refers to Islamic theological and legal doctrines, appearing in verses throughout the Qur'an and also in later Islamic sources. This expression defines the status of non-Muslims within Islamic communities. Jews, Christians and Sabaeans are people of the book, because they have inherited divine revelation and written it down as scripture. Unfortunately, from the Islamic perspective, these communities have gone astray and forgotten or distorted the original revelation (which Muslims have received once again, fully and finally, in its pure form). People of the book still have higher status, however, than those who reject the Qur'an. Islamic states allow them to maintain their religions, at least in theory, but charge them an additional tax. Some Islamic rulers tried to include Zoroastrians and even Hindus as people of the book, but they seldom succeeded for very long.

[47] Islamic theology recognizes no social or political distinctions when it comes to salvation and makes a point of demonstrating its universality in ritual settings such as the pilgrimage to Mecca. All male pilgrims adopt one costume and all women another.

[48] Bernard Lewis, *What Went Wrong: Western Impact and Middle Eastern Response* (New York: Oxford University Press, 2002).

[49] As a humanist, of course, I attribute the decline of Islam to the decline of its humanistic interpretations. What we would now call dictators seized control of Islamic regimes and used the spiritual and political authority of Islam for their own purposes. That situation prevails even today.

[50] Irshad Manji, *The Trouble with Islam Today: A Wake-up Call for Honesty and Change*, rev. ed. (Toronto: Vintage, 2005).

[51] Even the word "fundamentalist" was coined by Protestants to describe their own rebellion against liberal (secularized) forms of Protestantism in early twentieth-century America.

[52] I have focused my attention in this book primarily on the West, but my argument applies to the East as well. Hindu fundamentalism has emerged quite recently in India, mainly as a reaction against the secularism that was written into the country's constitution in order to create harmony among India's many religious and ethnic communities. Fundamentalist Hindus, represented by the Bharatiya Janata Party, believe that the government now gives more consideration to the needs of Muslims and other minorities than it does to those of the Hindu majority. They want a Hindu state for the Hindu majority, not a secular state. This would be a democratic state, but would it also be a humanist one?

[53] Paul Nathanson and Katherine K. Young, *Spreading Misandry: The Teaching of Contempt for Men in Popular Culture* (Montreal: McGill-Queen's University Press, 2001), 210, 219–220.

[54] The Nazis certainly set a new standard for murderous efficiency, but it would be false to claim that they were uniquely genocidal. Some Jews do make that claim (occasionally doing so even on metaphysical grounds), but they are wrong. The lamentable fact is that genocidal regimes had arisen before the Nazi regime and have arisen since the Nazi period. But not often, at least not in earlier centuries. Regimes that resort to mass murder of any kind are unusual enough to be classified separately.

[55] For a fascinating discussion of Egyptian philosophy, see Jan Assmann, *The Mind of Egypt: History and Meaning in the Time of the Pharaohs* (Cambridge: Harvard University Press, 1996).

[56] I refer here to the *very remote* past. Hunting-and-gathering societies in more recent times, such as those of Amerindians during the colonial period, were in a somewhat different position from their very early ancestors. For one thing, they coexisted and *traded* with agrarian Amerindians. Not surprisingly, they learned to store at least some surplus food and implements along their annual routes. As for the settled communities, some grew food and produced artifacts for themselves alone; others controlled the production of food and artifacts in vast empires. These peoples did not live in primeval wilderness; they lived in a world of boundaries and territories. Settled agrarians and nomadic hunter-gatherers interacted, sometimes peacefully and sometimes not, long before the arrival of Europeans.

[57] Egyptian women were probably freer and more respected than any other women in the ancient Mediterranean world, including Israelite women. Only one became a "king," Hatshepsut, but many queens were remembered with great respect and even love on public monuments. Ordinary women participated actively in commerce; they were not confined to the home. Joyce A. Tyldesley, *Daughters of Isis: Women of Ancient Egypt* (London: Viking, 1994).

[58] Egypt, on the other hand, was not a slave society; some captives became slaves, many of whom were household servants, but the economy as a whole did not rely on slaves. Even in the late, or imperial, phase of its history, Egypt relied primarily on paid peasant labor.

[59] It sounds counterintuitive to argue that the Southern Confederacy was both a slave state and a democratic one, but that is because "democracy" has taken on moral assumptions that are not inherent in the word. We often assume that democracies promote a familiar moral order, one that opposes any form of discrimination. Even in the past, not everyone made that assumption. The democracy that emerged in Britain and its colonies, for instance, took centuries to enfranchise everyone over the age of twenty-one. It took a long series of reform movements to enfranchise Jews, Catholics, men who did not own property, and women. For many years, moreover, the American constitution tolerated slavery. And it continued to tolerate racial discrimination for a hundred years after the Civil War ended slavery. Why did it take so long? Because every democracy—rule by the people (whoever they might be)—is only as morally aware as the *majority of its voters*. This is why democracies have taken measures, no matter how faltering, to *prevent* any tyranny of the majority. So, the South was a

democracy in the sense that it allowed some people—not all people, but some people—to vote for representatives in the legislatures. But some people could not vote. The main difference between Southern democracy and Northern democracy was that so many non-voters in the South were slaves. The difference was profound in moral terms but not in strictly political terms.

[60] The Magna Carta did very little for most people in England. By signing it, King John merely acknowledged some rights of his barons—that is, the aristocracy. Nonetheless, it inaugurated a process that would continue by diminishing royal rights and granting more and more rights to more and more segments of the population.

[61] Nathanson and Young, *Spreading Misandry*, 209–210.

[62] See Joseph Sassoon, *Self-Actualization* (Montreal: Humanica Press, 1988).

[63] Most Israelis are secular and many antireligious. It is true that religious Jews yearned for a return to the Holy Land. But that yearning had nothing to do with statehood, which is why many religious Jews were indifferent to statehood before the war and why a few religious Jews even now actually oppose the state of Israel. Religious Jews associate their return to the Holy Land with a messianic age, one that can exist only in the realm of eternity and infinity, not the creation of an ordinary state in the familiar realm of time and space.

Some early Zionists, such as Jabotinsky and Kook, were also religious Jews, but they did not create the state. It was secular Zionists such as Herzl who did that. They understood perfectly that a secular

Jewish state would be a state like every other state. That was precisely what they wanted it to be. Their whole theory of Zionism had as its goal the normalization of the Jewish people—that is, the reentry of the Jews into history after centuries of unnatural existence in ghettoes (and the resulting anti-Semitism). To do that, Jews needed a state, as did all other peoples. This state would be subject to all the normal social, economic, and political forces that affect every other state.

The state of Israel is secular, even though religious political parties have forced secular parties into alliances that compromise secularity—or, to put it another way, secular parties have found it politically expedient to make compromises of this kind. As a result, personal law for Jewish citizens (marriage, divorce, and so on) is guided by the *halakhah*. Other areas of law, though, are not.

Similar conflicts and compromises have entered American politics too. In both countries, the separation of religion and state is an embattled ideal. But it would be wrong to call either country a theocracy.

In view of the historical fact that every state has been temporary, and the scientific fact that nothing in nature endures forever, you could argue for the possible eternity of any state, including a Jewish state, only on theological or metaphysical grounds. You would have to ignore even biblical texts, moreover, which make it clear that God has already taken away two Jewish states and therefore might take away a third.

[64] Section 91 of Canada's Constitution Act of 1867 (also known as the British North America Act) mentions "peace, order and good government" as the essential principles of governance (which were thus equivalent to the American "life, liberty and the pursuit of happiness").

[65] Not all religions or even tendencies within the same religion agree on this. Mystical traditions, by definition, focus attention on union. Orthodox traditions set very clear limits on that, because one of their functions is to ensure communal survival and try to prevent people from becoming so absorbed in personal religious experiences that they ignore the needs of society in daily life. But every religion includes mystical and orthodox traditions.

Buddhism is primarily a mystical tradition, for instance, and Islam an orthodox one. Most Buddhists, nonetheless, live within larger societies beyond the monastic community (*sangha*), while any Muslim can become a mystic (Sufi). Hindus have another solution. They discourage young people from becoming wandering, mystical ascetics during a stage in the life-cycle that should be devoted to marriage, children, and community. Hindus encourage older people to experience mysticism after they have contributed to society as householders.

The extent of mystical experience, too, varies from one religion to another. Islamic and Christian forms of mysticism tend to complete union with the divine, but Judaism tends to isolated encounters with the divine.

[66] There is no such thing as a "humanist scientist," just as there is no such thing as a "Marxist scientist" or a "feminist scientist." There are only scientists, who search for truth—according to purely scientific principles—wherever that search leads them. You can believe in good faith that the search will lead every scientist to evidence that supports humanism, of course, but you cannot argue effectively that scientists per se can begin with a priori assumptions of *any* kind. People who begin with a priori assumptions are ideologues, not scientists.

[67] Even with the addition of laypeople, that would make scientists the new experts. And history—including that of Nazi Germany—shows that scientists are no more immune to malice than any other people. It could be argued that giving even more power to technocrats than they already have would make them the new ruling class. Humanists would have to avoid that danger.

[68] Leslie Lipson, *The Democratic Civilization* (New York: Oxford University Press, 1964).

[69] See Karl Polanyi, *The Great Transformation: The Political and Economic Origins of Our Time,* 2nd ed. (Boston: Beacon Press, 2001).

[70] Not all propaganda consists of lies—that is, *deliberate* deception. Some people produce propaganda out of sincere conviction, and even for causes that most of us would consider legitimate, as in the case of Hollywood movies that were intended to maintain American morale during World War II. The word *propaganda* itself originally referred to the propagation of an idea, and even now does not necessarily have a negative connotation. I have used it in this book, though, with the negative connotation that it has acquired in common parlance.

[71] According to Marxists of the Frankfurt School and their postmodernist followers, the covert propaganda that supports capitalist ideology is even more sinister than the overt propaganda that supports other ideologies. Their job has been to "deconstruct" the deceptions not only of advertisements and commercials but also of movies, songs, and other productions of popular culture in capitalist or "patriarchal" societies (but carefully avoiding any deconstruction of "subversive" or

"transgressive" popular culture or the popular culture of Marxist or non-Western societies). All of these things involve deception, they say, by presenting people with the illusion that capitalism or patriarchy is a benign system and thus hiding the oppressive reality.

[72] During the Spanish civil war, one of Franco's generals, José Millán Astray, was famously quoted as saying, "Death to intelligence. Long live death," during a confrontation with philosopher Miguel de Unamuno. (According to some witnesses, he said something more like "Death to traitor intellectuality.") Al-Qaeda and Hamas terrorists say the same thing. Their cause will ultimately win, they claim, because they prefer to die for their cause, if necessary, rather than to live on in intolerable circumstances.

[73] Although people have always asked this question, it was asked recently in a best seller: Harold S. Kushner, *When Bad Things Happen to Good People* (New York: Schocken, 1981).

[74] This, at any rate, is the answer that Job accepts, after rejecting many other answers. God gives him no explanation at all. Instead, God reveals his presence in a theophany. The depressing mystery of suffering, Job realizes, is nothing when compared to the joyful mystery of holiness.

Eastern religions have adopted very different approaches. According to the law of karma (*kamma*), suffering can be the just punishment for acts in earlier lives. Ultimately, though, suffering is an illusion.

To that Hindu explanation, the Buddha added his Four Noble Truths. According to the first, life itself is suffering (*dukka*). He did not mean that life is nothing but suffering, merely that everyone's life inevitably involves at least some suffering. According to the second, the cause of suffering is craving (*tanha*) for permanence in a world that is always in flux. When Buddhist philosophers analyzed that flux, they found that everything in the world consists of what we might call atoms that are continually combining, separating, and recombining in various patterns; the permanence of anything, therefore, is an illusion. According to the third, there is a solution to suffering. And according to the fourth, that solution is the Noble Eightfold Path: right living, right thinking, and so on.

[75] Viktor E. Frankl, *The Unconscious God: Psychotherapy and Theology* (New York: Simon and Schuster, 1975).

[76] See Joseph Sassoon, *Self-Actualization* (Montreal: Humanica Press, 1988).

[77] Democracies seldom fight each other for several reasons. For one thing, most people are reluctant to vote for those who would lead them into battle—except, of course, in self-defense. Moreover, most people in democracies value the rule of law, using negotiation and arbitration to settle disputes peacefully. Finally, war is expensive. World War I ended not because the Germans were inadequate soldiers but because the Germans ran out of money (and men) before their enemies did. After the war, even the victorious British and French found themselves so heavily in debt that they never recovered.

[78] Autocracies are by nature unstable, because they do not fulfill enough human needs of enough people. They antagonize the people through tyranny and deception, so autocrats must always worry about

coups and revolutions. One autocrat follows another without any appreciable difference for the people. It seldom gets any better; more often, it gets worse. The Russians rebelled against czarist tyranny but replaced that with Communist tyranny. Merely overthrowing an autocracy does not solve the problem, in short, unless democracy replaces autocracy.

[79] Many of these people really do want that as much as or even more than any other personal goal; they want history to remember them as semi-legendary heroes. I suspect that they have an unusual fear of death and see fame as a way of cheating it. The best example that I can think of is Hitler, but Kim Jong-un is probably another one.

[80] The problem of ends and means is by no means confined to autocracies. But the leaders of democracies rule by law. If they violate the law, they must face the anger of their people through the people's elected representatives.

[81] Every entelechial process is personal and therefore unique; no two people are exactly alike. They have common instincts, to be sure, but these lead to diverse behaviors. Humanists believe in free will. Everyone must make choices. This allows great diversity. Humanism does not lead to uniformity. Instead, it presents everyone with a road map that leads toward self-actualization.

[82] Joseph Sassoon, *Self-Actualization* (Montreal: Humanica Press, 1988).

[83] Abraham H. Maslow, *Toward a Psychology of Being* (New York: Van Nostrand, 1962), 15.

[84] Every state assumes a monopoly on violence, eliminating all other forms of violence as threats to itself, but some are stricter than others in maintaining this monopoly. Americans tolerate an extremely high rate of violence—much higher than that of any other democratic society and even many dictatorships—because, on the whole, they place an even higher value on the personal liberty to own a gun than they do on the collective need to ensure law and order. The Soviet Union, on the other hand, was both more and less violent than the United States. Every dictatorship is violent, because the state is founded on violence. Many thousands of Soviet citizens were brutalized in state-run concentration camps. But very few were brutalized by thugs in the streets.

[85] Americans are anomalous in this regard, too, because of their refusal to offer medical and other services as generously as other democracies or even some dictatorships. Moreover, they tolerate a relatively high rate of homelessness. These problems suggest that Americans place an even higher value on the liberty to get rich than they do on compassion for those who fail to earn any money at all. On a personal level, Americans are not selfish. On a collective level, though, something counteracts their generosity. They resist every intrusion on their personal liberty by "big government." Although the poorest Americans do receive free medical care, for instance, millions of middle-income Americans struggle desperately to pay their medical bills.

[86] Some modern dictatorships, on the other hand, have been very generous in this way. These states rule partly by threatening people with brute force but also, to a surprising degree, by convincing them to collaborate in their own oppression. Although many of the social services that we now take for granted originated in Bismarck's Germany,

Nazi Germany provided an even wider range of social services to its people (except, of course, to political dissenters and racial enemies). The Nazis did so partly to outdo the Communists, who had been their chief rivals. Like many people before and after them, most Germans were willing to make a deal with the devil. Hitler forced them to trade freedom and moral integrity for the promise of economic security, which he delivered. Something similar happened in the Soviet Union and its satellites. The Soviet state eventually succeeded in offering a wide range of social services to its people (except, once again, to political dissenters and those who were even suspected of getting out of line for any other reason). This explains why some people in post–Soviet Russia still feel nostalgia for the good old days under Stalin. He gave them very little freedom and maintained an economic system that generated very little wealth; on the other hand, he provided them with public education, pensions, medical care, and so on.

Contrasting the American system with the Soviet one, in particular, is instructive. Clearly, there is a price for everything. Americans enjoy unprecedented personal freedom, but one price of that is personal responsibility—which means, apart from anything else, that those who fail can blame no one but themselves and expect no one to bail them out. Soviet Russians enjoyed personal security as long as they conformed to the party line, but one price of that was induced passivity—which meant that they lost the ability to take responsibility for their own lives by making the many choices that democracy demands.

[87] Maslow called for the separation of reactions that are essential or good (constant D1) from those that are destructive (constant D2). "The difference [is] between the struggle, conflict, frustration, sadness, anxiety, tension, guilt, shame, etc. of the psychopathological person and

of the healthy persons. In the healthy person, these are or can be good influences." Abraham Maslow, *Motivation and Personality* (New York: Harper and Row, 1954), 366.

[88] With this in mind, consider the debate over creationism and evolution. As a humanist, I would evaluate creationism in connection with its implications in daily life for the entelechial process. I find that this principle, this axiom, does indeed support the entelechial process by promoting ideas such as the fatherhood of God, the brotherhood of man, and so forth. Therefore, it is an expression of true, or humanist, religion.

Darwin's theory of evolution, too, is legitimate to the extent that it supports the entelechial process. It does that by revealing scientific truth about nature (which is relevant to constant A4, which motivates people to seek truth about nature).

So, as a humanist, I see no contradiction between creationism as an unverifiable proposition and evolution as a verifiable one. One supplies morality and the second supplies scientific truth. Even if we could disprove evolution, that still would not confirm creation, because creationism and evolution represent very different motivations. Both are essential and synergistic. Both support self-actualization and the humanist cause.

[89] For a while, under the early Mughal emperors of India, Muslims interacted freely and happily with the conquered Hindus. Both Akbar and Dara Shukoh, for instance, were actively interested in Hinduism and other religions. Under later emperors, Hindus and other minorities in India did not fare so well.

INDEX

Totalitarianism, support of, 127*n*26, 127*n*27

Triumphalism, 22–23

Truth, 5

humanist journalism and, 77

Turkey, 48

U

Unified Theory of Motivation, 101–111

United States

democracy in, 14, 52–53

First Amendment, 49–50

foreign policy in, 49

humanist power in, 115–116

Supreme Court, 58–59

Universal Declaration of Human Rights, 41

Universalism, 17, 128*n*32

Upanishads, 24, 72, 93

V

Vandals, 21

Vatican Council, 22–23, 129*n*38

Vatican II, 12, 130*n*39, 130*n*40

Violence, 108, 143*n*84

Virtues, 17–18

Visigoths, 21

W

Wealth, redistribution of, 68

Women, 103, 105, 107–108

Egyptian, 35, 135*n*57

self-actualization of, 107

Z

Zionists, 136–137*n*63

Zoroastrianism, 47